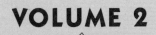

VOLUME 2

THE GLOBAL CLASSROOM

A Thematic
Multicultural Model
for the K-6 and ESL
Classroom

MICHELLE De COU-LANDBERG

Addison-Wesley Publishing Company, World Language Publishers

Reading, Massachusetts • Menlo Park, California • New York • Don Mills, Ontario • Wokingham, England • Amsterdam
Bonn • Sydney • Singapore • Tokyo • Madrid • San Juan • Paris • Seoul • Milan • Mexico City • Taipei, Taiwan

A Publication of Workd Language Publishers

Product Development Director: Judith M. Bittinger
Executive Editor: Elinor Chamas
Editorial Development: Clare Siska, John Chapman
Production/Manufacturing: James W. Gibbons
Cover, Text Design, and Production: Michelle Taverniti
Illustrations: Pamela Johnson, Michelle Taverniti
Cover Illustration: Paige Billin-Frye
Back Cover Photo: Judy Gulbis

Library of Congress Cataloging-in-Publication Data
De Cou-Landberg, Michelle, l934–
    The global classroom: a thematic multicultural model for
the K-6 and ESL classroom / Michelle De Cou-Landberg.
        p.   cm.
    Includes bibliographical references.
    ISBN 0-201-52759-6: $23.28. —ISBN 0-201-52960-2:
$23.28
    1. Multicultural education. 2. Education, Elementary—
Activity programs. 3. Language experience approach in
education. I. Title.
LC1099.D4 1994   93-48788
370.19′6—dc20   CIP

Printed in the United States of America on recycled paper.

ISBN: 0-201-52960-2
1 2 3 4 5 6 7 8 9 10 CRS 98 97 96 95 94

This book is dedicated to children around the world, particularly to young refugees who are innocent victims of war and violence.

Twenty percent of the author's royalties will go to the Tibetan Children's Village in Dharamsala, India.

ACKNOWLEDGEMENTS

Preparing a book for publication is like preparing for the birth of a child. Many people support the idea and your efforts, but only a few give generously of their time and advice.

Dr. Esther Eisenhower was one of these people. I am immensely appreciative of all the support and encouragement she has given me and greatly indebted to her for her constructive criticism upon reviewing the first draft of my book.

My warmest thanks go to Dr. Donna Kay Wright, who supported my efforts as a teacher and contributed the Foreword to this book. I would also like to express my gratitude to Erik Pursehouse, Courtney Pelley, and Frank Bensinger, most enabling administrators, and to my former teachers—Mademoiselle Beaumont, Mademoiselle Hugon, Madame Lucette Desvignes, and Monsieur Jean Talon—for their understanding instruction and guidance.

I appreciate the important contributions made by my colleagues. Jim Blair, Alice Bransfield, Donna Carpenelli, Cynthia Eckert, Soon Kee Falkenstrom, Pam Freer, Franna Ruddel, and Joanne Schilling contributed materials and creative ideas to the book. Audrey Van Vliet and Carol Williams were also kind enough to take time out of their busy schedules to read materials and offer suggestions.

The Global Classroom would never have seen the light of day without the wonderful Addison-Wesley team, and I owe a debt of thanks to Judith Bittinger, who first listened to my ideas, and to Elinor Chamas, Clare Siska, John Chapman, Evelyn Nelson, and Calvin Wang for their enthusiastic support from start to finish.

I would like to express my filial gratitude to my mother and father, whose courage and compassion remain a daily source of inspiration for me.

I am immensely indebted to my family for their help: to my husband, Erik, for his patience and support; to my daughter, Claire, for her suggestions and practical ideas; to my son, Michel-David, who inspired the segment on aviation; and most of all to my son, Jacques-Frédéric, who taught me how to use my computer.

My deep love and gratitude go out to all my students—past and present—for sharing their affection, their cultures, and their talents with me. Special thanks go to Daysi and Evelin Abarca, Caleb Anzoleaga, and Jennifer Arevalo for their artwork, and to Stanislava Uhrik for her poem, "Peace."

My students' collective gift, for which I am most grateful, is that they have afforded me glimpses into the true nature of the human condition and shown me the courage of children in the face of adversity.

Michelle De Cou-Landberg
Reston, Virginia

CONTENTS

LIST OF REPRODUCIBLES

The pages listed here may be reproduced for classroom use.

FOREWORD

When I accepted a position as principal of Haycock Elementary School in 1980, I expected to be greeted by the kinds of students found in most suburban Washington, D.C. neighborhoods. I soon discovered, however, that Haycock was not a typical suburban school. It had been designated a magnet school for the county's ESL program. The children came from all over the world and spoke 15 different languages. Some of their parents were from diplomatic families, while others had reached the U.S. via refugee camps where they had experienced horrors most people cannot even imagine.

How could we meet the special needs of such a diverse ESL population and, at the same time, help the native speakers in the school gain from this unique opportunity to learn more about the world? The answer to this question came from an exceptional ESL teacher, Michelle De Cou-Landberg. She devised completely original lessons based on the needs and resources of each student.

But Michelle did more than just teach English. She arranged a presentation on Japanese writing for the whole school. She organized the production and sale of an international cookbook and put together a Children's International Festival. Her activities helped students, parents, and teachers to understand and appreciate more deeply each others' cultures.

The Global Classroom contains the essence of what Michelle brought to Haycock. It is full of classroom suggestions, but it also contains many ideas for bringing together ESL students, non-ESL students, teachers, families, and the community in an environment that will help everyone learn to live and work together. I commend Michelle for her extraordinary service to children from all lands and cultures and for her contribution to the growth of global education.

D. Kay Wright
United States Department of Education
Mid-Atlantic Region

INTRODUCTION

*T*he *Global Classroom* is child-centered.

- It provides for a setting in which all contributions are valued and all experiences are meaningful.
- It seeks to develop a supportive environment in which the student is nurtured and develops a positive self-image.
- It helps children learn about, appreciate, and celebrate the differences and the commonalities of the world's many cultures.

The Global Classroom consists of two volumes. Volume 2 contains four chapters, each of which addresses a universal theme: clothing, housing, transportation, and celebrations. Each chapter provides a wide variety of exercises to capture students' interest, expand their language abilities, motivate them to read, and show them how to share the learning process with their families. All activities can be used in a variety of settings and can be adapted to a wide range of age and proficiency levels. Volume 1 of *The Global Classroom* follows a similar format and includes chapters on weather, plants, animals, and food.

Chapters 1 through 3 of Volume 2 follow a set format. The first four sections of these chapters (Sparking Interest, Expanding Language, Reading and Reflecting, and Creating and Sharing) contain activities and strategies which address the issues of multi-level grouping, classroom management, and collaborative learning. The fifth section, Getting Families Involved, gives suggestions for helping include students' families in the education and acculturation process. The sixth section, Suggested Readings, contains a listing of multicultural children's books which focus on the chapter theme. The last section of each chapter contains reproducible masters which can be duplicated for classroom use.

Sparking Interest

In the Sparking Interest section you will find suggestions for generating interest in the theme. Considerable aural and visual materials are used so that students have a chance to listen and watch. They are also encouraged to use the senses of touch, smell, and taste as ways of getting to know more about the theme.

Expanding Language

In this section, activities focus on building vocabulary, improving pronunciation, and figuring out how the grammar of English works. All activities grow out of the context provided by the chapter theme, and all classwork involves real, meaningful communication.

Reading and Reflecting

In this section, students take a look at some books relating to the theme. Big Books are often used at the beginning of this section to provide a whole-group reading activity. Then, beginning level students may listen to the teacher read stories and respond by drawing a picture or writing a few words. More advanced students may read on their own in groups. Specific books and follow-up activities are listed along with original projects.

Creating and Sharing

In this section, students work on art projects, do further research into some aspect of the theme, write or deliver oral reports, publish booklets, and carry out hands-on science projects.

Getting Families Involved

The suggestions in this section have several purposes. One is to let the family know what the student is learning so that they can provide emotional support. A second purpose is to draw on the resources students' families can provide for the class as a whole. When family members share aspects of their culture (such as food, art, or music) with the class, all students are drawn closer together and communication is enhanced. A third function of these suggestions is to give non-English-speaking family members some exposure to the language.

Suggested Readings

Each chapter ends with a list of theme-related titles which can be used to expand and enrich activities. A diamond (♦) appears next to any title which is also featured in the chapter. These featured titles are not required readings, but are used to illustrate the literature-based activities. You may wish to substitute another book related to the theme from this list, or from your classroom or library collection.

Reproducibles

Reproducible masters which accompany some of the suggested activities are found throughout the book. Teachers are encouraged to use the ideas presented in these reproducibles to construct new versions tailored to the needs of a particular class.

The material in Volume 2, Chapter 4, Multicultural Celebrations, utilizes an innovative format which ties together all the themes presented in Volumes 1 and 2 of *The Global Classroom.* Students learn about the foods, games, customs, and languages of other countries and plan a multicultural celebration involving other children in the school as well as family and community members. This chapter features a Global Calendar of Celebrations and an alphabetically organized list of multicultural activities which children can learn about and then present to their guests.

All four chapters provide a wide variety of choices from which you can construct your own sequence of instruction. Many of the activities can be applied across the themes, adapted to different levels of students, and built upon or recreated by you or your students. You may choose to spend as little or as much time on any section or theme as you wish, integrate and expand activities, or become inspired to create entirely new activities. The material is presented as a springboard for creativity, with the needs and interests of your students as your guide.

In the margin of each page you will find three types of entries: Notes, Materials, and Readings. The Notes provide special insights and suggestions for expanding on an activity. A Materials list is provided when an activity requires materials beyond those commonly found in the classroom. Reading lists highlight the books featured in literature-based activities. (Detailed publication information for these books can be found in the Suggested Readings section of each chapter.)

The materials presented in *The Global Classroom* reflect the author's experiences as a French student learning English as a "living language" (langue vivante); as an EFL teacher in France and Laos; as an observer of literacy projects in Nepal and schools in India; and as an ESL teacher in Fairfax County, Virginia. There are more activities here than any teacher could ever cover in one school year—activities to help you teach exciting, inviting, child-centered classes. Feel free to pick and choose, to imitate, to innovate. Use *The Global Classroom* not only to teach English, but also to celebrate the cultural diversity of your students.

CLOTHING OF MANY COUNTRIES

Chapter

1

REBOZO, KURTA, AND SAROUEL

CONTENT AREA LEARNING WEB

CLOTHING OF MANY COUNTRIES

SCIENCE

Experimenting with sounds, 4–5
Experimenting with dyes, 20
Discussing climate and clothing, 20

MATH

Making a graph, 28–29
Comparing prices, 30

LANGUAGE ARTS

Consonant blends, 8
Compound words, 8
Alphabetical order, 9
Homonyms, 11
Minimal pairs, 11
Possessives, 11
Antonyms, 12
Compound adjectives, 12
Researching word origins, 12
Building descriptive vocabulary, 22
Learning about similes, 27
Researching color words, 28

FAMILY INVOLVEMENT

Sharing booklets with family members, 6
Discussing native country clothing, 7
Sharing a story with family members, 14
Contributing to comparative linguistics charts, 28
Teaching the class how to weave or make a quilt, 29
Modeling special clothing, 29
Setting up a clothing exchange, 29
Completing a shopper's survey, 29

SOCIAL STUDIES

Displaying dolls from many countries, 4
Showing national costumes, 4
Studying Native American weaving, 18
Discussing culture and clothing, 20–21
Making a timeline, 27
Planning an international trip, 28
Researching crop growth, 28

ART AND MUSIC

Making clothing booklets, 6
Ceremonial clothing, 7–8
Making puppets, 13
Drawing pictures of hats, 16–17
Making a fabric bear, 23
Making a storybook, 26
Making a fabric sample book, 26
Making posters, 27

READING COMPREHENSION

Listening to stories, 4
Introducing fables, 4, 16
Looking at characters, 13
Choral reading, 14
Comparing two stories, 14
Using Venn diagrams to compare stories, 14–15
Using a flow chart, 18–19
Reader's theater, 22
Making a comparative literature chart, 22–25

CHAPTER 1. CLOTHING OF MANY COUNTRIES

Just as the range of choices in a typical box of crayons has expanded well beyond the eight primary colors, modern clothing employs a vast array of shades and materials and styles. Moreover, the tags attached to the clothes we wear reveal an astonishing diversity of origin, representing nearly every nation in the world.

This explosion of color and variety is particularly noticeable in schools on special days such as United Nations Day, Chinese New Year, and *Id al-Fitr*. Even stronger than the bold colors is the pride in their cultural heritage displayed by students, a feeling which you will be able to nurture. Special occasions also provide excellent opportunities to take a fresh look at the map, to reinforce our sense of history, to convey acceptance of diversity, and to send a clear message that all clothes are beautiful, regardless of their style or condition.

A unit on clothing seems to appeal to students of all ages and levels. It is well-suited to activities which will promote the acquisition of basic and/or advanced vocabulary. It enables students to formulate grammatical rules as they dabble in linguistics, and it gives them an opportunity to integrate social studies and math with language. Finally, the chapter gets family members involved and helps reinforce pride in each student's cultural heritage.

إلي ماله أم كأنه
ثوب بدون كم

A person without a mother is like a dress without a sleeve.

—ARABIC PROVERB

SPARKING INTEREST

This part of the chapter is designed to get students thinking about clothing—both their own and that of others. You will be able to present them with a wide variety of visual, auditory, and tactile experiences which will provide some surprises and help stimulate their natural curiosity.

MATERIALS

✔ dolls from a variety of foreign countries

MATERIALS

✔ magazines and catalogs
✔ postcards and posters
✔ photographs of students in national costume

MATERIALS

✔ clothes and accessories worn in foreign countries

Using Visual Stimuli

● Set up a display of dolls from many countries in one corner of your room, or in a public place in the school. Ask students to look them over and bring to class any questions or comments they may have.

● Have students fill the bulletin board with a variety of clothing pictures including photographs of themselves in their national dress, pictures cut out of magazines and catalogs, and post-cards and posters of people wearing unusual clothing. Invite them to cut out anything that catches their interest. Encourage students to spend some time at the board talking with others about the pictures there.

● Turn part of the room into a *souk* or bazaar, exhibiting clothes from all around the world. Start by putting out a few items that you own or are able to obtain from acquaintances. Then encourage students to add to the collection. Watch how fast it grows!

● Wear clothing from a different country to class each day. A male teacher might wear a *kurta* from India, a *guyabera* from Central America, or an embroidered shirt from the Philippines. A female teacher might wear a vest from Guatemala, a blouse from Portugal, or a skirt from India (featuring bold red and green colors). She might carry a purse made from *kente* cloth. Use your imagination and ingenuity to locate clothing from a variety of foreign countries and watch your students' eyes sparkle with delight and appreciation.

Using Auditory Stimuli

✔ The Emperor's New Clothes *(any version)*
✔ Caps For Sale, *by Esphyr Slobodkina*
✔ Mufaro's Beautiful Daughters, *by John Steptoe*

READING

● Read aloud some of the following books. Encourage students to ask questions and make comments about the stories. Use this opportunity to ask them to relate clothing-related fables or folktales from their countries of origin.
The Emperor's New Clothes
Caps For Sale, by Esphyr Slobodkina
Mufaro's Beautiful Daughters, by John Steptoe

● Ask your students to close their eyes and listen to the clicking of high heels or tap shoes, the muffled sound of sneakers, and the flip-flop of rubber sandals on the floor.

- Hang a flag or pennant outside your classroom window and listen to it flapping in the wind.
- Have students make sounds using various kinds of fabrics. They can make rustling sounds with silk, buzzing sounds with corduroy, ripping sounds with velcro fasteners, snapping sounds with towels, etc.

Using Kinesthetic Stimuli

- Pass around an alpaca sweater and a silk scarf so that students can feel the softness of the alpaca hair and the silkiness of the scarf. Ask students to describe what each one feels like and record their comments on the board.
- Distribute samples of unprocessed wool and ask students to comment on what the texture is like and what the wool smells like.
- Pass around the stem of a cotton plant with the bolls still attached so that students can touch and smell unprocessed cotton. Discuss the process of removing the cotton from the plant and making it into the fine, smooth cloth we like to wear.

MATERIALS
✓ *samples of a wide variety of fabrics*

MATERIALS
✓ *items of clothing made from alpaca and silk*

MATERIALS
✓ *samples of unprocessed wool and cotton*

EXPANDING LANGUAGE

Teaching the vocabulary of clothing is probably the easiest task of all. Just think! All the props are lined up in front of you: striped T-shirts, solid-color jeans, fancy dresses with polka dots, and on special days, special clothing. You will see billowing *salwars* tightly gathered at the ankle, a graceful *ao-dai* floating on a slender Vietnamese girl, and caps and vests made of African *kente* cloth in colorful patterns.

Activities for Beginning Students

Introducing Vocabulary. Once children can answer basic questions pertaining to their immediate needs and can handle classroom routines such as asking permission, obtaining supplies, and understanding directions, they will be able to gain a considerable amount of language and self-confidence from a unit on clothing. Use realia and/or pictures to introduce and practice new vocabulary items. Model all questions and answers. Use the "Say and Do" technique. For example, point to a boy's T-shirt as you ask, *What is this?* and model the answer: *This is a T-shirt.* Have students repeat each sentence as they touch the appropriate item of clothing.

Expanding Vocabulary and Syntax. Add new words and sentence structures in small increments. For example, you might move on to the patterns: *What are these?/These are...* and *What color is this?/It's...* Reinforce vocabulary and syntax with a brief daily review. You can expand sentence types by having an advanced level student come to the front of the room and describe what he or she is wearing today. Introduce other personal pronouns by asking one student to point to another student (or students) and describe the person's clothes using *he, she, we, you, and they.*

***Introducing* Adjective + Noun.** When students have mastered the present progressive form of the verb *wear* and basic articles of clothing, you can add colors. Use your judgement as you gradually increase the difficulty of the questions. A beginning student may find it useful to practice highly repetitive sentences: *I am wearing a blue shirt. I am wearing a brown belt.* More advanced students could be encouraged to create longer statements such as: *I am wearing a striped shirt. You are wearing a dress with red polka dots. Salvador is wearing tan pants and a blue shirt with long sleeves. We are all wearing sneakers.*

In French and Spanish the adjective follows the noun. Students who speak these languages will benefit from extra word order practice.

N O T E

Making Clothing Booklets

- Catalogs and magazines provide an endless supply of free materials. Make simple booklets by folding a piece of 8½-by-11-inch construction paper in half. Have students cut out and paste in pictures of boys, girls, men, and women wearing different types of clothes. Help students write labels (*a blue shirt, red shorts*) and simple descriptions (*He is tall. She has short blond hair.*). Encourage students to share the booklets with class members and their families.

- Invite students to use the same materials to make up booklets in which they sort the clothes into such categories as sportswear, swimwear, hats, footwear, and jewelry. Help them label each page and show them how to use a picture dictionary to find words they don't know. This is a good activity to introduce them to the concept of classifying, and students can follow up on the activity by writing simple sentences about some of the items, for example: *The bracelet is gold.* and *The necklace is long.*

Activities for Intermediate Level Students

Expanding Vocabulary

● Ask students to draw and label pictures of clothing worn on festive occasions in their country (or region) of origin. Make this a homework assignment so that family members can be involved. Encourage students to display and discuss their completed pictures in class using the first language term as well as the English equivalent.

● Talk about some of the differences in clothing customs around the world. Here are some questions you might ask

This Laotian ceremonial skirt is called a sinh.

MATERIALS

✓ *bolts of cloth*
✓ *items of clothing*
✓ *butcher paper*
✓ *crayon or marker*

during class to develop language and start the discussion: *Do you take off your shoes when you enter your house? What do you wear on your feet? When do you wear a raincoat? Do women usually wear skirts or dresses? Do men usually wear long pants or shorts? In what places do you cover your head? What do you wear to sleep in? Do you ever carry an umbrella? Did you wear a school uniform in your country? in your previous school?*

Looking at Consonant Blends. Use the topic of clothing to introduce (or review) the use of consonant blends. Set up a small table displaying some bolts of cloth and some remnants. Hang a sign over it saying *CLOTH.* Set up a rack nearby with various articles of clothing hanging from it. Label it *CLOTHING.* Give students a list of consonant blends and have them work in groups to make up a list of clothes utilizing these sounds. With the whole class, revise the list, printing it in alphabetical order on a large piece of paper. Post it on the bulletin board. You may wish to add your own lists of words that start with consonant blends.

Using Compound Words. This thematic unit on clothing also provides plenty of opportunities for students to recognize compound words and learn how to separate the two components. Depending upon your students' abilities, you might ask them to do some of the following.

- Brainstorm a list of compound words related to clothing.

- Divide each compound word into its separate components.

- Illustrate some compound words, either realistically or in a humorous manner as in the drawing below.

Sun + Dress = Sundress
Evelin Abarca, Age 11

CLOTHES

a blazer
a blouse
a bracelet
a dress
a glove
a scarf
a shawl
a shirt
a shoe
shorts
a skirt
slacks
a slip
a slipper
a smock
a sneaker
a snowsuit
a stocking
a sweater
trousers

CLOTH

checks
floral
plaid
print
striped

Clothes or Cloth?

- Write the words in alphabetical order.
- Match up a scrambled list of first and second halves. For example, one list might have words like *ear* and *bath,* and the other words like *ring* and *robe.* More advanced students could even make up quizzes like this for each other. You'll find some words to get you started in the illustration on the next page.

bathrobe
buttonhole earring
eyeglasses handbag
handkerchief
necktie
nightgown overalls
overcoat
pocket book
raincoat

shirttail
shoelace snowsuit
sundress
sunglasses
sweatshirt
turtleneck
underwear
waistband
windbreaker

MATERIALS

✓ three large boxes
✓ clothing, including some pairs of items
✓ jeans, pants, trousers, or shorts
✓ clothesline
✓ butcher paper
✓ marker

A, An, A Pair or Several?

● Teach the concept of *a pair* using real objects. Ask students to bring in items of clothing from home and borrow items from the Lost and Found at school. Place three large boxes at the front of the room, label box 1 *a/an,* label box 2 *a pair,* and label box 3 *several.* Supply model language as you place items in various boxes. Then mix up all the items and ask students to sort them out into the three boxes, describing what they are doing as they do it. (For example, in box 1 you might have a belt and a hat. In box 2 you might have a pair of gloves and a pair of socks. In box 3 you might have three bracelets and four blouses.) Discuss the use of *a pair* and help students formulate some rules about it. Post a list of pairs which students can add to whenever they wish.

● Some pairs are not made up of two separate objects. Use this list to help teach about pairs of things that come in one piece, not two: jeans, pants, trousers, slacks, shorts, and tights. Point out that items of clothing similar to pants (with separate coverings for each leg) and eyewear (with a separate lens for each eye) are referred to as *pairs,* while shirt-like items (with a separate covering for each arm) are not referred to as pairs.

NOTE

Try putting up a clothesline and giving students the sensory experience of hanging things in pairs.

Discovering Homonyms. Use words such as *plain, sew,* and *blue* as opportunities for students to formulate a list of homonyms in their notebooks. Here are a few to start with: *blue/blew, red/read, dear/deer, sale/sail, high/hi, seam/seem, new/knew, sew/so, heel/heal* and *sole/soul.*

Looking at Minimal Pairs

● Some ESL students experience difficulty with words such as the following, which present very slight differences in pronunciation: *collar/color, cuff/cough,* and *loose/lose.* Do an oral minimal pair activity in class. Say pairs of words and ask students to say *same* if they think you have said the same word twice (*collar, collar*), and *different* if the two words do not sound exactly the same (*collar, color*). As you continue to play the game, students' ability to hear the differences will gradually improve.

● Here are some other clothing words you could use for further practice with minimal pairs.

Initial Position	Final position	Vowels
cheap / sheep	tight / tied	cap / cup
vest / best	neat / need	sack / sock
shoes / choose	lace / lays	hat / hot

Using Possessives

● Students who come from language backgrounds in which the possessive is formed by constructions that use the word *of* (producing word-for-word translations such as, *the dress of Jane,* or *the sweater of my brother*) may need extra help with the English possessive system. The clothing theme lends itself particularly well to a mini-lesson on possessives. Introduce the basic rules: Use 's with singular nouns and irregular plurals (*the boy's shoe, the child's hat, the people's coats, the children's boots*); use only the apostrophe for plurals ending in *s* (*the Smiths' clothes, her parents' raincoats*).

● To practice possessives, ask each student to think up one sample sentence and write it on the blackboard. Students love the opportunity to write on the board. Discuss each example, pointing out what each student got right and inviting each contributor to correct his or her own sentence, if necessary. This way no egos will be bruised and everybody

✓ *"Possessives" reproducible master, page 33*

will have a chance to shine and to learn. Make copies of the "Possessives" exercise on page 33 and ask students to complete it. Go over the results individually with each student.

Activities for More Advanced Students

Discovering Antonyms. Introduce students to some of the following antonyms relating to clothing, and see how many more they can come up with. Ask them to keep lists in their notebooks. Start with: *heavy/light, dark/light, plain/fancy, wide/narrow, neat/sloppy, loose/tight, expensive/cheap, casual/dressy, dull/gaudy, coarse/smooth. stiff/limp,* and *brand-new/threadbare.*

Using Compound Adjectives. This activity can serve as the starting point for a continuing exploration of compound adjectives. Make a list on a large sheet of paper and post it on the wall. Throughout the rest of the chapter, students can add to the list as they discover new compound adjectives. Start with these examples: *high-heeled, short-sleeved, well-groomed, dry-cleaned, long-sleeved, double-breasted, well-dressed, ready-made, machine-made,* and *man-made.*

Studying Word Origins

- This section closes with pictures that contain some linguistic comparisons. These drawings point out similarities among languages and make clear the phenomenal exchange of ideas (including modes of dress) that have taken place over the centuries around the world. Guided by you, students will think about these articles of clothing—their origins, their usefulness, and the materials they are made of. At the same time, they will be able to trace linguistic connections that have bridged a wide variety of geographic areas.

- Make copies of "What Do You Call It?" on pages 34–35 and give a copy to each student. Then discuss the items, one at a time. Point out that the word *shawl* is similar in all the languages shown. If a student speaks one of the languages shown, ask him or her to pronounce the word and say something about who wears shawls and why. Conduct a similar activity for the jacket and sandal pictures. Then ask students to make a colored drawing of one of these articles of clothing and to share it with the class.

The time and effort it takes to fill your classroom with objects, pictures, photographs, charts, etc. is a very good investment. These elements help students internalize concepts and pass from the concrete to the abstract. The colorful items you bring to the class enable students of all ages and levels to participate more fully in the learning process.

READING AND REFLECTING

Like a Matrioshka doll set which reveals one gaily-painted motif after another, a thematic unit on clothing unveils theme under theme, topic within topic. The abundance of available materials makes choosing difficult, but the good news is that you can choose which topics are most appropriate and timely for presentation to your students. Below are descriptions of some of the stories and activities I have used. You can use this summary to come up with your own ideas for how to make use of the clothing-related books that are available to you.

Activities for Beginning Level Students

Looking at Characters

READING

✓ Mrs. Wishy-washy, by Joy Cowley

MATERIALS

✓ posterboard
✓ newsprint
✓ markers
✓ tongue depressors
✓ glue
✓ laminating materials

- Read aloud the Big Book, *Mrs. Wishy-washy,* by Joy Cowley. You'll find that there is nothing "wishy-washy" about Mrs. Wishy-washy, a large, energetic woman who wears distinctive clothes—a turban, a pleated blue dress, a red and white apron, and huge, fuzzy slippers. Her stance, hands on hips, reveals her firm resolve.

- Invite students to draw pictures of Mrs. Wishy-washy, the Cow, the Pig, and the Duck on sketching paper or posterboard and color or paint each one. Then ask them to cut them out and glue them on tongue depressors to use as puppets. Laminate them, if possible, and use them as you introduce the concept of characters. Turn a bulletin board into a stage by draping a curtain around the edges. Invite students to draw in a setting using newsprint and crayons. Later you can change the setting and have students create new characters from other stories.

✓ Caps for Sale, *by Esphyr Slobodkina*
✓ Topiwallah *(anonymous)*

✓ The Gingerbread Man *(any version)*
✓ Little Round Bun *(any version)*

✓ *"Topi Pattern" reproducible master, page 37*
✓ *construction paper*
✓ *newsprint*
✓ *crayons or markers*

● Conduct a choral reading of the book. The availability of small books is another asset, since youngsters can borrow them and share the funny story with their families.

Comparing Two Stories

● The two books, *Topiwallah* and *Caps for Sale,* by Esphyr Slobodkina, give students the opportunity to develop their critical thinking skills by comparing and contrasting two versions of the same story. *Caps for Sale,* a tale from Eastern Europe, is available in Big Book and small book format so students can share it with family members. I like to have children act out the Indian version of the story, *Topiwallah.* It is also interesting for them to see the Devanagari alphabet and writing system in the book.

● Experiment with selecting your own pairs of books and establishing your own parallels between two versions of any story, be it in Tagalog, Tamaheq, Tamil, or English.

● *The Gingerbread Man,* another favorite, also exists in a Russian version, Little Round Bun, which provides an opportunity for you to make interesting comparisons between two versions of that story.

Doing More with Two Stories

● Act out the story of *Topiwallah* by dressing as an Indian peddler wearing a *topi* and carrying a bundle on one shoulder. (You can find a "Topi Pattern" on page 37.)

● Brandish red, pink, and yellow paper topis and encourage students to guess the names of the colors in Hindi. Then tell them the answers. (For example red is *lal.*) Then read the story in Hindi, and contrast the Devanagari alphabet with the Roman alphabet. Ask students to guess which countries such a story might take place in.

● Show the cover of *Caps for Sale* and compare the peddler to the Topiwallah, and topis to caps. Then read *Caps for Sale,* list new vocabulary words on blackboard, and ask students to use the words in sentences.

● Ask students to contribute information as you draw a Venn diagram like the one shown here on the blackboard or on newsprint. In a Venn diagram, the material that applies to each story individually is placed in the left side of the left

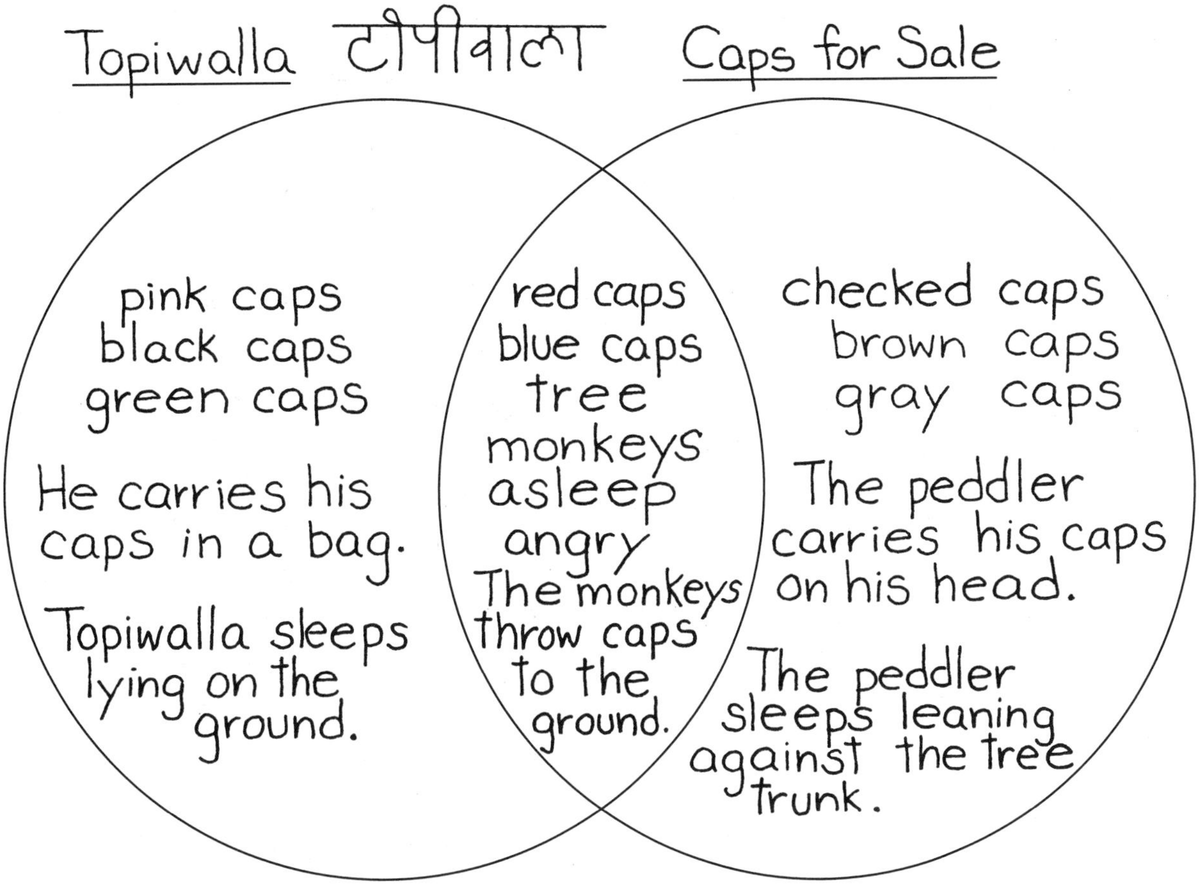

Topiwalla टोपीवाला Caps for Sale

Topiwalla (left circle):
pink caps
black caps
green caps

He carries his caps in a bag.

Topiwalla sleeps lying on the ground.

Both (center overlap):
red caps
blue caps
tree
monkeys
asleep
angry
The monkeys throw caps to the ground.

Caps for Sale (right circle):
checked caps
brown caps
gray caps

The peddler carries his caps on his head.

The peddler sleeps leaning against the tree trunk.

A Venn Diagram Comparing Topiwallah *and* Caps for Sale

hand circle and the right side of the right hand circle. Material that applies to both stories goes in the central, overlapping portion of the two circles. Students can then use the diagram to discuss the stories, their similarities, and their differences.

Following a Character through Two Stories

✓ Corduroy, *by Don Freeman*
✓ A Pocket for Corduroy, *by Don Freeman*

R E A D I N G

● *Corduroy* and *A Pocket for Corduroy,* by Don Freeman, are stories about a teddy bear which always seem to win young students' hearts. These books can be used with more than one level of students. You can emphasize the basic vocabulary and reinforce the structure *He is wearing...* with beginners, while more advanced students can talk about fabrics, department stores, getting lost, and friendship.

● Since the pocket is a prominent feature of Corduroy's overalls, it might lead to a discussion of what students can carry in their pockets.

✓ *piece of corduroy fabric*

- Bring a sample of corduroy fabric and have students start a list of fabrics in their notebooks which they can add to as they continue reading.

- A follow-up activity for *Corduroy,* featuring a cutout, is outlined on page 23.

Activities for Intermediate Level Students

Introducing Fables

✓ City Mouse and Country Mouse *(any version)*

- *City Mouse and Country Mouse* is a popular story that makes a good introduction to fables. The version I use comes in booklet form and uses a controlled vocabulary, thereby making the story easy to read. The story can also be found in a number of basal readers, and lends itself well to a discussion of the terms *character, setting,* and *moral of the story.*

✓ *newsprint*
✓ *crayons or markers*

- As a prereading activity, ask students to brainstorm some advantages and disadvantages of living in the city and the country. Use a large sheet of newsprint so that all students can see the words as you add them.

- Present the two mice as sympathetic characters and the cat and dog as the villains. A pantomime or dramatization of the story allows beginning level students to be included in the process. More advanced students can discuss characters, describe physical features and attributes, and talk about the moral of the story.

Looking at Human Nature

✓ Uncle Nacho's Hat, *adapted by Harriet Rohmer*

- Another delightful tale with a message is *Uncle Nacho's Hat,* or *El Sombrero del Tío Nacho,* adapted by Harriet Rohmer, which is presented in a bilingual version and is available on audio cassette. Although his old hat is full of holes, Uncle Nacho is very attached to it, and he finds it hard to discard even after his young niece, Ambrosia, presents him with a new one. The Puppet Workshop of Nicaraguan National Television uses this tale to illustrate how some people cling to old habits and resist change.

- Ask students to reflect on the various functions of hats. A sombrero creates shade and keeps the hot sun off a person's head. What else do hats do? Suggest that students draw pictures of various types of hats and write a few words about their function.

Sympathizing with a Character

- *The Umbrella Thief,* by Sybil Wettasinghe, provides another view of the innovative ways in which people deal with progress and its problems. One day Kiri Mama experiences the surprise of his life when he visits a big city and discovers that people there do not carry banana or yam leaves to protect themselves from the elements, but huge flower-shaped things. Intrigued and fascinated, he picks out an umbrella which he brings back to his village. To Kiri Mama's immense disappointment, the umbrella vanishes. Youngsters are always moved by the artist's marvelous depiction of Kiri Mama's drooping mustache and huge, sad, black eyes under the banana leaf which he must now use to protect himself from the rain.

- Capitalize on the animated classroom discussion which follows the reading of this book and ask students to describe similar experiences in their own lives. These responses can then be placed in a collective book in the shape of an umbrella.

- Another activity can involve the retelling of the story featuring a different ending.

- Some of the best follow-up activities can come from your students themselves. Ask them to brainstorm a list of things to do with the story and help shape these suggestions into interesting classroom projects.

Following the Plot

- *A New Coat for Anna,* by Harriet Ziefert, used in Volume 1, Chapter 1 to illustrate the cycle of seasons, can also be used to demonstrate the steps in transforming wool into an article of clothing. Less advanced students will enjoy *From Cotton to Pants* and *From Sheep to Scarf* (both by Ali Mitgutsch) for parallel reading.

- Discuss systems of *trade, exchange,* and *barter* and encourage students to provide real-life examples.

- Show the cover of *A New Coat for Anna* and invite students to make predictions about the story, based on title and book cover.

- Read the book, list students' responses, and record the stages in the fabrication of Anna's coat. Discuss and explain new vocabulary as necessary. Create a word bank.

- Invite lower-proficiency students to draw pictures of their favorite parts of the story and, if possible, write a few sentences about them.

- Use the cycle of events in the story to teach students how to design flow charts. This particular graphic organizer enables students to follow the sequence of events, select the most salient details, and learn how to write concise, meaningful sentences.

- The flow chart on the next page is the product of the collaboration of two third-graders, one Spanish-speaking with one year of instruction in English, the other French-speaking with eight months of instruction. After I discussed the format and modelled the first steps on the blackboard, they eagerly took over. After they had their writing conferences with me, they typed the edited sentences into the computer. I revised this work so that it would fit into the blocks they had designed. The last step was cutting out the various blocks and gluing them in the right position.

Reading Stories about Weaving

- The weaving tradition in the Southwest, especially among the Navajo, provides us with a wide selection of clothing-related books about Native Americans. *The Goat in the Rug,* by Charles Blood and Martin Link, tells about Geraldine the Goat. At first she is unwilling, but later she is proud to participate in the creation of a rug woven by Glenmae, the Navajo weaver. Ask interested students to locate pictures of Navajo weavings in encyclopedias or art books and to share them with the rest of the class.

- *Little Herder in Autumn,* by Ann Nolan Clark, is written in English with a Navajo translation. The story depicts the world of a young Navajo girl, her relationship to her family, to animals, and to nature. It also shows the various steps in the weaving process. Some students may wish to make a Venn Diagram contrasting this story with *The Goat in the Rug.* (Venn diagrams are described on pages 14–15.)

MATERIALS

✓ drawing paper
✓ markers
✓ word-processing equipment
✓ scissors
✓ paste

READING

✓ The Goat in the Rug, *by Charles Blood and Martin Link*
✓ social studies books and art books

READING

✓ Little Herder in Autumn, *by Ann Nolan Clark*

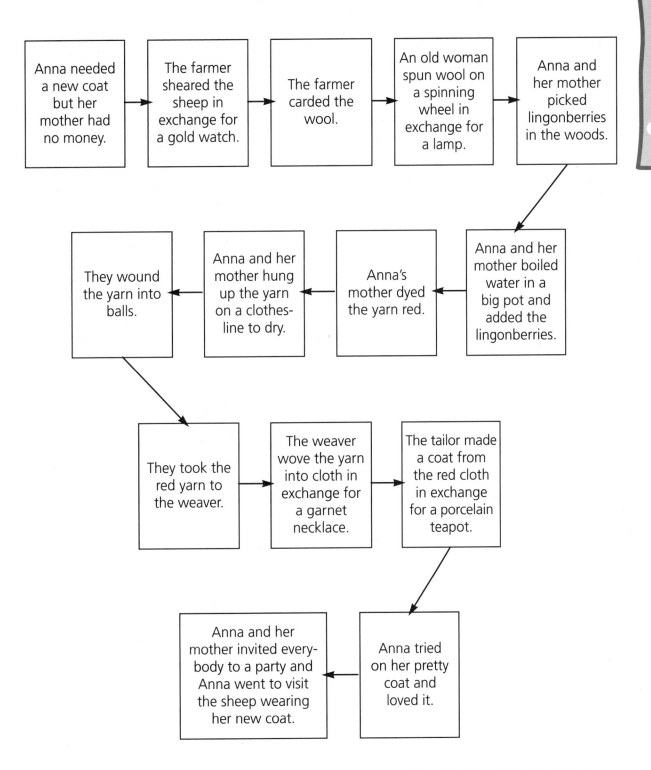

Flow Chart for A New Coat For Anna

✓ Annie and the Old One, *by Miska Miles*
✓ The Enchanted Tapestry, *retold by Robert D. San Souci*

✓ *berries, beets, and other natural dyes*
✓ *worn-out white sheeting*
✓ *hot water*

- *Annie and The Old One,* by Miska Miles, is a must-read. This story can be compared and contrasted with *The Enchanted Tapestry,* a Chinese folktale retold by Robert D. San Souci. Once again we can see the advantage of a global classroom—it has no borders.

- This also might be a good time to do some experiments with dyes using natural products like berries and beets. Crush each coloring substance and mix it with hot water. Have students dip strips of cloth in the mixture and then place them on the windowsill to dry. Compare the dry colors with the original colors.

Activities for Advanced Level Students

An obvious advantage of thematic units such as those presented in this book is that you can link up a variety of topics with each other and focus on themes within themes. The following suggestions show how you can help students expand their reading on the topic of clothing in many different directions.

Making a Social Studies Connection. As students begin reading about a specific country in social studies, point out that clothing is a basic need largely dictated by climate and the availability of local resources, or of trade with the outside world. Provide students with a framework of questions and strategies to guide them in their reading. Begin with questions such as these: *What are people in the pictures wearing? What do you think clothes there are made of? Are there special hats, veils, or headdresses? What clothing-related crops are grown there?*

Seeing Clothing as a Reflection of Culture

✓ Nine-in-One Grr! Grr!, *retold by Blia Xiong*
✓ Tonight Is Carnaval, *by Arthur Dorros*
✓ Just Plain Fancy, *by Patricia Polacco*

- Look at how clothing reflects the culture it comes from. In *Nine-in-One Grr! Grr!,* a Laotian legend retold by Blia Xiong, the vivid, stylized embroidery on the Great Shao's clothes, the silver coins used as ornaments, and the majestic headdress worn by the Shao's wife are typical of the clothing worn by the Hmong tribes in Laos. They are reminiscent of the *arpilleras* of Peru used by Arthur Dorros to illustrate *Tonight Is Carnaval.* Patricia Polacco's *Just Plain Fancy* provides a contrast to the explosion of striking colors in these two books. The simple, practical designs and soft colors of the Amish clothing reflect the austerity of their lifestyle.

- Discuss with students how the clothing of a culture tells you something about the character of the people. Ask them to draw pictures of the variations that exist for a certain item of clothing (such as the hat) in the different cultures presented in the above (or other) stories. Encourage them to share their drawings with other students.

Identifying Very Special Clothing

- Ask students to talk about their favorite item of clothing. It may be a new baseball cap, a cozy pair of slippers, or an old pair of jeans. Point out that sometimes the most special piece of clothing in a person's mind is something he or she doesn't own. Then read and discuss some of the following stories, or other stories about special clothing.

- In the story *Down, Down the Mountain,* by Ellis Credle, Hank and his sister, Hetty, lived in a log cabin in the Blue Ridge Mountains and longed for the day when they would be able to wear "creaky-squeaky" shining shoes. They eventually earn the money to buy them.

- The hero of *The Most Beautiful Place in the World,* by Ann Cameron, has much in common with the children in the previous story. He lives in the mountains, has a wise, loving Granny, and is willing to work hard to get the shoes he so badly wants.

- On the other side of the world, the main character of *A Cap for Mul Chand,* by Julie Forsyth Batchelor, an eleven-year-old boy living in a small Indian village, wants to buy a cap so he can visit his uncle in Bombay. He, too, overcomes obstacles to get the clothing he wants.

- *The Hundred Dresses,* by Eleanor Estes, is about prejudice and cruelty between children based on the fact that some of them can afford fancy clothes and some of them can't. The story ends with a victory of forgiveness and compassion over cruelty and cowardice, and this is a story that students will not soon forget.

- *The Patchwork Quilt,* by Valerie Flournoy, tells a story about a special use for worn out clothing. A quilt, begun by Grandma and finished by young Tanya, is made from patches of clothing that bring back memories and reflect the deep love and affection between members of the family.

✓ *dictionaries*

✓ The Emperor's New Clothes *(any version)*

✓ Under the Carambola Tree, *in* Look What We've Brought You from Vietnam, *by Phyllis Shalant*

- Call out the names of the books you have read and ask children to raise their hands for their favorite. Ask the children to form groups based on their favorite story. Suggest that each group list their reasons for liking that book best. Later, ask each group to share its list of reasons with the rest of class.

- Ask each student to choose one of the stories and to write down all of the words used to describe the clothing in the story. Ask them to find out the meanings of any words they don't know from the dictionary or from a classmate. Then have them look at the pictures and try to add other words that the author could have used. Go over these lists with each student.

Seeing Clothing as a Status Symbol

- *The Emperor's New Clothes* always amuses children and serves as a perfect lesson on the perils of vanity. Ask some students to present a reader's theater version of the story. More advanced students can read the story aloud, taking the roles of narrator, king, subjects, etc. Some less advanced students can be assigned roles and pantomime the story as it is read. This gives less able readers a chance to review the story and to participate fully in a classroom activity without being put on the spot.

- *Under the Carambola Tree,* presented as a play by Phyllis Shalant in her book *Look What We've Brought You from Vietnam,* illustrates how differences in status shown by clothing have nothing to do with the inner goodness of the person. After reading the story, ask students to describe the kind of clothing that the rich and famous wear in their native countries. Compare and contrast the types of clothing that convey status in different countries.

Using Clothing as a Disguise

- Children and adults alike find it intriguing to pretend they are someone else. Halloween, *Fasching,* and *Carnaval* are festivals with pagan or religious roots in which masks feature prominently. However, in the following books, clothing as a disguise represents more than a form of entertainment. It is used as a disguise to conceal identity and to save lives.

- In *The Upstairs Room,* by Johanna Reiss, one of the heroines, Sina, has to dress as a farm girl, while her ten-year-old sister,

Annie, wears a sailor suit to escape from some Nazis in pursuit of Jews in occupied Holland during World War II.

- In *The Night Journey,* by Kathryn Lasky, Nana Sashie tells her great-granddaughter the story of her ordeal as she and her family escaped from Russia disguised as Purim players.

- Ask students to help you complete a Venn diagram on a large piece of paper comparing and contrasting *The Upstairs Room* and *The Night Journey.* Follow the format outlined on page 14 for *Topiwallah* and *Caps for Sale.*

Using a Comparative Literature Chart

- Finally, you might consider comparing and contrasting several versions of the popular fairy tale *Cinderella,* focusing on the clothes worn by Cinderella as a key element in the story. Tell students a little bit about each version of the story you are able to obtain, and let them decide which ones they would like to read or listen to.

- On the following pages is a Comparative Literature Chart which helps students organize and compare a variety of data about the various versions of the *Cinderella* story including the clothing, the slippers, and the dress worn by the heroine as an indication of her new status. Put the column headings on the board and help students get started by filling in the information on the first story together. Then ask them to complete the rest of the chart on their own.

CREATING AND SHARING

Choosing from the wide array of projects outlined here may be a challenge. You can choose to do a few of them exactly as they are outlined, or you can use some of the ideas as springboards for projects of your own.

Activities for Beginning Level Students

Making Models of a Favorite Character

- Reread *A Pocket for Corduroy* with the class. Then show students how they can make their own fabric teddy bears. Hand out copies of the "Corduroy Doll Pattern" on page 36. Provide students with scraps of felt for the body and corduroy

TITLE	AUTHOR	ILLUSTRATOR	COUNTRY	PERIOD	
Kongjee Patjee (Korean Cinderella)	edited by Edward B. Adams	Dong Ito Choi	Korea	a long time ago	
Cendrillon	Charles Perrault	Diane Goode	France	17th century	
Princess Furball	Charlotte Huck	Anita Lobel	England	The Middle Ages	
Moss Gown	William H. Hooks	Donald Carrick	U.S.A.	18th century	
The Egyptian Cinderella	Shirley Climo	Ruth Heller	Egypt	6th century B.C.	
Yeh-Shen	Ai-Ling Louie	Ed Young	China	Táng dynasty (618–907 A.D.)	
Tam and Cam	Alice M. Terada	Janet Larsen	Vietnam	a long time ago	

NAME OF HEROINE	DRESS	SHOES
Kongjee	silk dress, hair tied with ribbon	bright red shoes
Cendrillon (in French "cendre"="cinder")	gown of silk, lace, and pearls	high-heeled glass slippers
Furball	glittering gold dress, coat of 1,000 furs	no mention
Candace, "Moss Gown"	moss and rags gossamer gown	no mention
Rhodopis ("rosy-cheeked")	plain tunic	rose red slippers with gold on toes
Yeh-Shen	azure blue gown, Kingfisher feather cloak	Slippers with golden thread, solid gold shoes
Tam	peach-colored dress, yellow blouse, black pants, green scarf, orange scarf	white silk shoes with precious stones

Comparative Literature Chart—Cinderella Stories

✓ *"Corduroy Doll Pattern"* reproducible master, page 36
✓ scraps of felt and corduroy fabric
✓ colored markers, scissors, and paste

for the overalls, and have them cut out the two shapes using the outlines on the reproducible as a guide. They can paste the overalls on the bear and use colored markers to add facial and other features, including a pocket and a button. Remember that Corduroy had one missing button!

● A fabric teddy bear of their own is a powerful incentive for students to write a story, or at least a description of what they have created. Encourage students to write whatever they wish, using the experience of making their own teddy bear as a starting point.

Making a Storybook. After rereading *Topiwallah,* ask students to use their imaginations and make up a story about a hat. Edit their work and ask them to make a final copy for publication. You can make the project especially attractive by giving each student a copy of the "Topi Pattern" on page 37 and having them use the pattern to cut out a book cover (of cardboard) and pages (of plain or lined paper), both of which are shaped like the *topi* hat in the story. The book can be bound by punching holes along one side of the cover and pages, and using string or yarn to sew it together.

✓ Topiwallah *(Anonymous)*

***Celebrating* Hat Day.** Declare a new holiday—Hat Day. Have students design their own hats made out of construction paper or bring in caps, sombreros, veils, and other sorts of headgear worn in various foreign countries. Encourage students to describe the hat they are wearing and to ask questions about other people's hats.

✓ *"Topi Pattern"* reproducible master, page 37
✓ cardboard and paper
✓ yarn

Making a Fabric Sample Book. Cut pieces of construction paper in two and staple them into a book in which students can glue leftover pieces of fabric they have at home or can get from friends and relatives. Label each sample and display the book so everyone can look through it.

Activities for Intermediate and Advanced Level Students

✓ construction paper
✓ paste
✓ markers
✓ hats from foreign countries
✓ various fabric samples

Making Commercials. Students can develop one-minute commercials for various articles of clothing. As they prepare, help them focus on key selling points and provide models of pronunciation and intonation as necessary. Invite them to

✓ videotaping equipment

present their commercials in front of the class or on video, if available.

Making a Timeline. This is a good group activity. First the group uses recycled computer paper (or other paper that is at least six feet long) to create a timeline to put up on the wall. It should show dates from 500 B.C. to the present in 100-year intervals about three inches apart. Individuals can then choose one or more types of historical dress (metal armor, wooden shoes, etc.) and research when and where people wore this type of clothing and how it was made. Each person reports back to the group. Then they can make drawings of their items of clothing on plain paper and place them on the timeline. Ask the group to explain their timeline to the rest of the class and to answer questions about it.

Making Posters. Using any book they have read (including social studies books, art books, storybooks, etc.), ask students to design posters illustrating the costumes people wore during the time period presented in the book. For example, after reading the version of *Cinderella* translated and illustrated by Diane Goode, a student might make a poster of several types of court dress worn by both men and women in 17th-century France. Other students could use the regular catalog or the *Treasures of Tutankhamun* catalog from the Metropolitan Museum of Art in New York to create a poster after reading *The Egyptian Cinderella.*

Learning about Similes

- Have students look back at the stories listed on their Comparative Literature Chart (pages 24–25) and make lists of similes used in each one. First explain that *similes* are descriptions that compare one thing to another using the word *like* or *as.* For example, *She runs like the wind* is a simile that means that the person runs very fast. Here are some examples from the books mentioned earlier in this chapter:

• *The Egyptian Cinderella*	Their skin glowed like copper. Her feet sparkled like fireflies. Her eyes are as green as the Nile.
• *Yeh-Shen*	Her feet felt light as air.
• *Cendrillon*	She ran as swiftly as a frightened deer.

MATERIALS
✓ computer printouts with one clean side
✓ markers
✓ transparent tape
✓ reference and history books

MATERIALS
✓ publications showing historic clothes or jewelry
✓ large drawing paper
✓ crayons or markers

Packing Your Suitcase. This activity combines research and writing. Have students imagine that they are going to take a trip to a faraway country of their choice, or that they are going to visit relatives in their home country. Have them make a list of clothes that they will need to pack. Then make a second list of the clothes and accessories that they might like to buy there to bring back to friends in the United States. (A Russian student might need to pack a warm parka and a Guatemalan student might want to bring back an embroidered blouse for a friend.) Ask students to find out how shoe and clothing sizes are determined in their target country and to figure out the sizes of clothing they would need to buy.

Giving Individual and Group Reports

- Ask students to work alone, in pairs, or in small groups to research and present reports on one or more of the following topics.

  - Where did these color names come from?

  Find out the origins of the words *coral, emerald green, mocha, Nile green, ruby red, saffron, salmon, terra cotta,* and *turquoise.*

  - Where did these clothing names come from?

  Find out the origins of the words *jodhpurs, khaki, kimono, oxfords, knickers,* and *raglan sleeve.*

  - Who produces the most cotton (or wool or silk)?

  Use an encyclopedia or social studies book to look up current production of a certain fabric. Then make a pie chart or a line graph to illustrate your findings. (A sample chart is shown on the following page.)

GETTING FAMILIES INVOLVED

As always, try to involve families as much as possible. This unit on clothing provides plenty of opportunities for family members to be part of the teaching process. They may contribute to comparative linguistics charts, provide information on which clothes to take on a trip to a specific country, and assist in determining which system is used to measure sizes. Family members may be

Production of Cotton (1993)

MILLIONS OF BALES

China	🌸🌸🌸🌸🌸🌸🌸🌸🌸🌸🌸🌸🌸🌸🌸🌸🌸🌸🌸	19,300,000
U.S.A.	🌸🌸🌸🌸🌸🌸🌸🌸🌸🌸🌸🌸🌸🌸🌸	15,400,000
India	🌸🌸🌸🌸🌸🌸🌸	6,800,000
Pakistan	🌸🌸🌸🌸🌸🌸	5,560,000
Brazil	🌸🌸🌸🌸	3,290,000
Turkey	🌸🌸🌸	2,550,000
Egypt	🌸🌸	1,600,000
Mexico	🌸🌸	1,300,000

🌸 = 1,000,000 bales

willing to show the class how to make *arpilleras,* how to weave, or how to make a quilt. They may even be able to demonstrate how to wrap a *sari,* to describe the various articles of *hanbok* clothing worn in Korea, or to model how to don a *chèche* (the seven-meter-long piece of gauze worn in North Africa for protection against the sun, wind, and sand of the Sahara desert).

One useful way for a school to reciprocate for all these useful services is to hold a Clothing Exchange at certain times of the year, preferably at conference time. Members of children's families may swap their outgrown children's clothes for larger sizes and recycle clothes they can no longer use. Since the practice of recycling used clothing may not be familiar to some students, you may have to explain how the system works and why it is such a wonderful way to share with others.

The final project in this chapter is a Shopper's Survey, which involves teamwork between family members and child. Make a copy of the "Shopper's Survey" on page 38 for each student in your class. Go over the survey before having students complete

✓ *"Shopper's Survey"*
reproducible master,
page 38

it with their families. Allow time in class for students to compare their completed surveys with those of other students. Find out what materials various items of clothing are commonly made from, which countries produce them, which stores charge the most, and how much prices vary from store to store.

CONCLUSION

Common threads run through this unit on clothing and reinforce the theme of interconnectedness which is the cornerstone of *The Global Classroom*. Pictures from catalogs, a display of clothes from many cultures, and the visual stimulation offered by multicultural books all provide learning opportunities for students. They get practice in making comparisons, conducting research, using critical thinking skills, and reflecting and writing about their experiences. They also have a chance to involve family members at all stages.

SUGGESTED READINGS

(Titles mentioned in this chapter are marked with a ♦.)

♦ Adams, Edward B. *Korean Cinderella.* Seoul, Korea: International Publishing House, 1982.

Addison-Wesley Publishing Company. *The Addison-Wesley Picture Dictionary.* Reading, MA: 1984.

♦ Batchelor, Julie Forsyth. *A Cap for Mul Chand.* New York: Harcourt Brace & Co., 1950.

♦ Blood, Charles L. and Link, Martin. *The Goat in the Rug.* New York: Macmillan Publishing Co., 1990.

♦ Cameron, Anne. *The Most Beautiful Place in the World.* New York: Alfred A. Knopf, 1988.

♦ Clark, Ann Nolan. *Little Herder in Autumn.* Santa Fe, New Mexico: Ancient City Press, 1988.

♦ Climo, Shirley. *The Egyptian Cinderella.* New York: Thomas Y. Crowell, 1989.

♦ Cowley, Joy. *Mrs. Wishy-washy.* New York: Doubleday, 1990.

◆ Credle, Ellis. *Down, Down the Mountain.* New York: Lodestar Books, 1934.

  Daly, Niki. *Not So Fast, Songololo.* New York: Puffin Books, 1987.

◆ Dorros, Arthur. *Tonight Is Carnaval.* New York: Dutton, 1991.

◆ Estes, Eleanor. *The Hundred Dresses.* New York: Scholastic, 1973.

◆ Flournoy, Valerie. *The Patchwork Quilt.* New York: Dial Books for Young Readers, 1985. (Reading Rainbow Book, Coretta King Award)

◆ Freeman, Don. *A Pocket for Corduroy.* New York: Viking Press, 1978.

◆ ———. *Corduroy.* New York: Viking Press, 1968.

◆ Hooks, William H. *Moss Gown.* Boston: Houghton Mifflin, 1987.

◆ Huck, Charlotte. *Princess Furball.* New York: Scholastic, 1989.

◆ Lasky, Kathryn. *The Night Journey.* New York: Puffin Books, 1986. (ALA Notable Book, National Jewish Book Award)

◆ Louie, Ai-Ling. *Yeh-Shen, A Cinderella Story from China.* New York: Philomel Books, 1982.

◆ Miles, Miska. *Annie and the Old One.* Boston: Little, Brown and Co., 1971.

◆ Mitgutsch, Ali. *From Cotton to Pants.* Minneapolis: Carolrhoda Books, 1981.

◆ ———. *From Sheep to Scarf.* Minneapolis: Carolrhoda Books, 1981.

  Newton, Pam. *The Stonecutter.* New York: G. P. Putnam's Sons, 1990.

◆ Perrault, Charles. *Cinderella.* New York: Alfred A. Knopf, 1988.

◆ Polacco, Patricia. *Just Plain Fancy.* New York: Bantam Books, 1990.

◆ Reiss, Johanna. *The Upstairs Room.* New York: Thomas Y. Crowell, 1972. (Newbery Medal)

  Rodanas, Kristina. *The Story of Wali Dâd.* New York: Lothrop, Lee & Shepard Books, 1988.

♦ Rohmer, Harriet. *Uncle Nacho's Hat / El Sombrero del Tió Nacho.* San Francisco: Children's Book Press, 1989.

♦ San Souci, Robert D. *The Enchanted Tapestry.* New York: Dial Books for Young Readers, 1987.

———. *The Talking Eggs.* New York: Scholastic, 1989.

♦ Shalant, Phyllis. *Look What We've Brought You from Vietnam.* New York: Simon & Schuster, 1988.

♦ Slobodkina, Esphyr. *Caps for Sale.* New York: Scholastic, 1987.

♦ Steptoe, John. *Mufaro's Beautiful Daughters.* New York: Scholastic, 1987. (Caldecott Honor Book)

♦ Terada, Alice M. *Under the Starfruit Tree.* Honolulu: University of Hawaii Press, 1989.

♦ *Topiwallah* (anonymous). Delhi, India: Delhi Bureau of Textbooks, 1970.

♦ Wettasinghe, Sybil. *The Umbrella Thief.* Brooklyn, New York: Kane/Miller Book Publishers, 1987.

♦ Xiong, Blia. *Nine-in-One Grr! Grr!* San Francisco: Children's Book Press, 1989.

♦ Ziefert, Harriet. *A New Coat for Anna.* New York: Alfred A. Knopf, 1986.

ADDITIONAL RESOURCES

Smallwood, Betty Ansin. *The Literature Connection: A Read-Aloud Guide for Multicultural Classrooms.* Reading, MA: Addison-Wesley, 1991. (This annotated guide to multicultural literature lists additional titles in its section on Clothing/Body, Pages 110–113.)

POSSESSIVES

Name_____ Date _____

Change each of the phrases below into a possessive using **'s** or just an apostrophe (**'**).Then write a complete sentence using the new possessive form.

1. The cap of the man _____

_____

2. The umbrella of father _____

_____

3. The shoes of the boys _____

_____

4. The raincoats of her children _____

_____

5. The sneakers of the boy _____

_____

6. The sweater of my brother Hugo_____

_____

7. The dress of my mother _____

_____

8. The clothes of the ladies _____

_____

9. The jackets of the men _____

_____

10. The blouses of the women _____

_____

WHAT DO YOU CALL IT?

Shawl

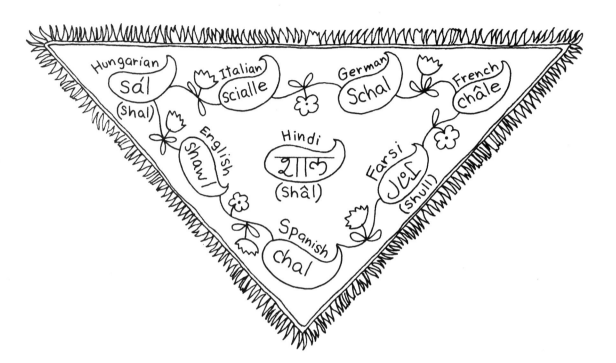

Sandal

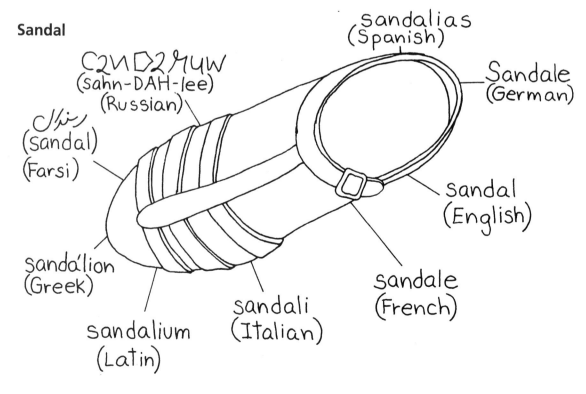

WHAT DO YOU CALL IT?

Jacket

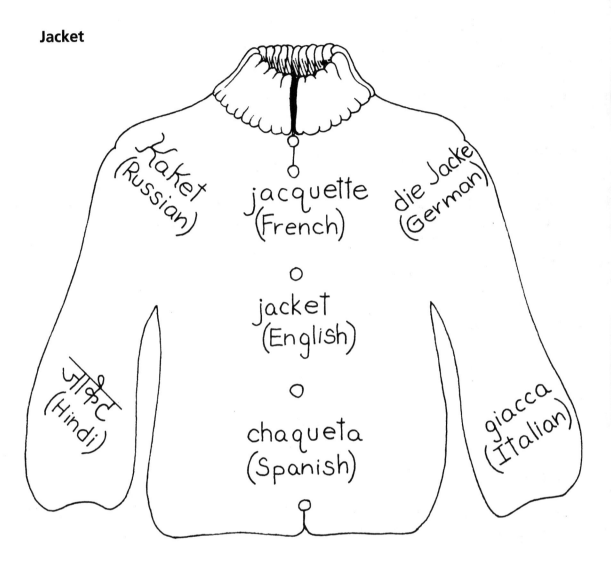

куртка
(Russian)

jacquette
(French)

die Jacke
(German)

o

jacket
(English)

o

जैकेट
(Hindi)

chaqueta
(Spanish)

giacca
(Italian)

35

CORDUROY DOLL PATTERN

TOPI PATTERN

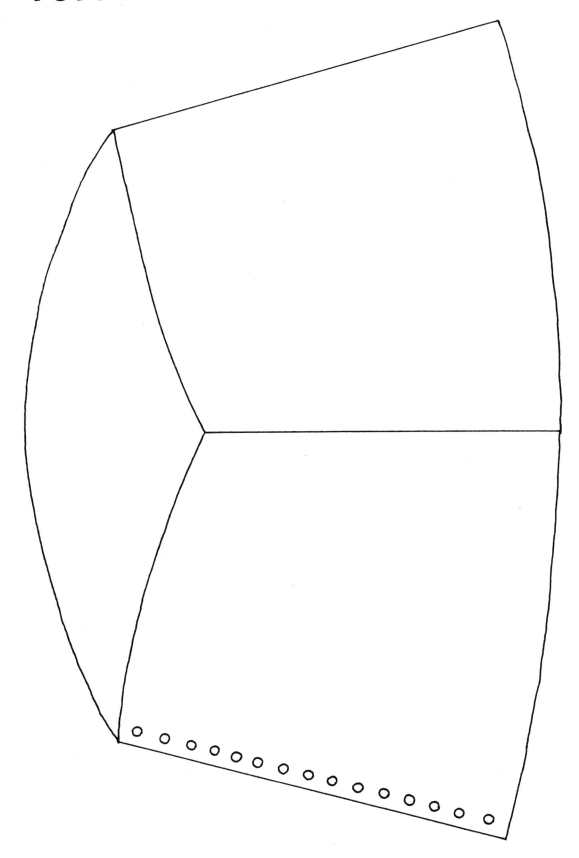

SHOPPER'S SURVEY

Store	Item	Price	Material	Made in

1. Take this paper and a pencil and go to a mall or a clothing store.

2. Try to find similar items of clothing in several different stores.

3. Write the name of the store, the name of the item, its price, the material it is made from, and the country where it was made.

HOUSES AROUND THE WORLD

Chapter

2

ROUND, SQUARE, AND ON STILTS

CONTENT AREA LEARNING WEB

HOUSES AROUND THE WORLD

CHAPTER 2. HOUSES AROUND THE WORLD

낙숫물이 댓돌을 뚫는다.

Raindrops falling from the roof will cut through stone.

—KOREAN SAYING

Of the eight thematic units presented in *The Global Classroom,* Volumes 1 and 2, the unit on houses will probably stir up the deepest emotions in the hearts of your students. Some families willingly left behind security and a pleasant lifestyle in order to see what else life had to offer. Others are refugees from places of sadness and terror. No matter why children came to leave their homelands, many carry their share of tears or scars.

Modest though their dwellings may have been—a bamboo house perched on stilts, a mud hut with a palm leaf roof, a smokey shanty without a chimney—these dwellings represented more than a roof over the child's head. They signified home, shelter, family, community, and country. If the children were old enough to remember, the smells, sounds, and sights associated with their first homes will stay with them forever. A sense of homelessness may haunt some of them for many years. And yet, out of this dramatic upheaval, an indomitable spirit will emerge: a resilience and a determination to survive hardships and to excel.

The first two sections of this unit will awaken students' interest, provide strategies for vocabulary building, and introduce the concept of home as a shelter for animals as well as people. Based on their own experiences and on class discussions and research, students will begin to develop solid inferential skills. They will begin to understand how the weather affects people's lives. They will also learn to analyze the physical features of houses and other buildings, and see how they relate to the geography, climate, and resources of the country where they are found.

SPARKING INTEREST

This section contains a variety of activities designed to make your students more conscious of the many different types of houses and homes people live in. They will take another look at

MATERIALS

✓ postcards
✓ magazines
✓ scissors
✓ personal photographs

READING

✓ books about houses
✓ local newspapers
✓ home improvement magazines

READING

✓ Giorgio's Village, by Tomie de Paola
✓ Look Inside a House, by Denise Patrick

READING

✓ A House Is a House for Me, by Mary Ann Hoberman
✓ The Village of Round and Square Houses, by Ann Grifalconi
✓ The Indian and His Pueblo, by Louise Lee Floethe

their own homes, read about houses in several different countries, and even fantasize about the dream house they might build someday.

Using Visual Stimuli

- Ask students to contribute to a class bulletin board featuring as many types of houses as possible. Encourage them to bring in postcards, magazine clippings, personal photographs, and original drawings of houses from around the world. Take some time each day to discuss any additions to this display.

- Put together a collection of reading material on housing and display it in the Book Corner. Include books about houses, real estate sections from local newspapers, brochures advertising new housing developments, and a collection of home improvement magazines.

- Invite students to close their eyes and visualize the houses they left behind in their native countries. Suggest that they think about such details as what the roof looked like, what shape the windows were, and what kind of plants grew nearby. Ask volunteers to share their visual images with the rest of the class.

- Show the class some picture books about houses. Two good ones to start with are *Giorgio's Village*, a pop-up book by Tomie de Paola, and *Look Inside a House*, by Denise Patrick.

Using Auditory Stimuli

- Read aloud some Big Books or play audio cassettes of books about houses. Three books of interest to students at all levels are: *A House Is a House for Me*, by Mary Ann Hoberman, *The Village of Round and Square Houses*, by Ann Grifalconi, and *The Indian and His Pueblo*, by Louise Lee Floethe.

- Students may benefit from hearing a given book more than once. Sometimes they are able to comprehend a great deal more the second time around, which can be very encouraging.

Using Kinesthetic Stimuli

- Take a walk around the neighborhood, looking at the types of housing that are available. Point out single-family homes, apartment buildings, trailers, apartment hotels, etc. When you get back from your walk, list the various types of houses children saw on a large piece of paper.

- Invite students to draw, sketch, or paint pictures of the houses they left behind in their native countries, the houses they are living in now, or their dream houses.

✓ What it Feels Like to Be a Building, *by Forrest Wilson*

READING

- Share with students the book *What it Feels Like to Be a Building,* by Forrest Wilson. Place a padded exercise mat on the floor and encourage children to act out some of the stresses and pushes experienced by various parts of the buildings described in the book.

EXPANDING LANGUAGE

Now that students know what the unit is all about, they are ready to begin expanding the range of vocabulary and grammatical structures they can use to talk about the topic. This section contains activities that are appropriate for all ability levels.

Activities for Beginning Level Students

Drawing a House

- As soon as you return from your walk around the neighborhood, discuss with the class the types of houses you have seen. Even beginning level and newly-arrived students will be able to contribute words and ideas to the discussion.

In many countries what Americans call the "first floor" is called the "ground floor." The "second floor" is then called the "first floor."

NOTE

- Then draw a house (or have a student draw one) on posterboard and label the main parts as shown in the drawing on page 44. Ask students to compare it with the house or apartment they live in now, or another place they have lived.

Making a Paper House

- Hand out the necessary materials and ask students to make paper models of a house like the one in the drawing. Show them how to measure and cut out windows and doors, and encourage them to draw on shutters, roofing patterns, and exterior siding of boards or brick.

MATERIALS

✓ construction paper
✓ rulers
✓ scissors
✓ markers
✓ transparent tape

- Ask students to ask and answer questions about their houses using *There is* and *There are.* They might have exchanges,

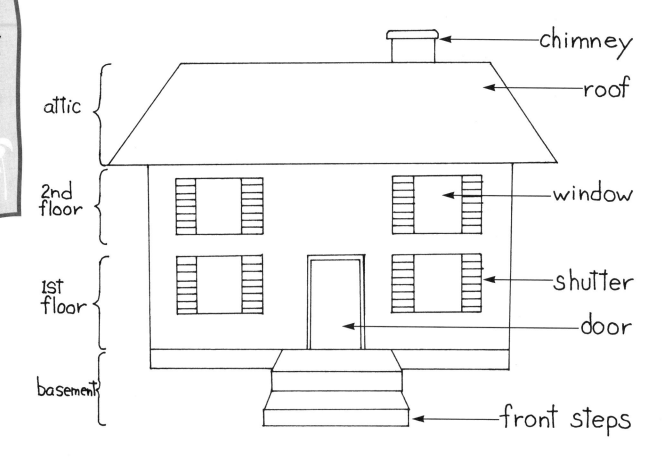

attic

2nd floor

1st floor

basement

chimney

roof

window

shutter

door

front steps

such as *Are there any windows?* (Yes, there are.) *Is there a chimney?* (No, there isn't.)

Drawing a Floor Plan

- Once students have mastered the names of the exterior parts of the house, discuss the various rooms found inside a house: kitchen, dining room, living room, bedroom, bathroom, and family room. Draw a simple floor plan on the board and label the rooms. Add a few pieces of furniture (such as a table in the dining room and a bed in the bedroom).

- Then ask children to make similar diagrams of the house or apartment they are living in. When they have finished, ask them to share their drawings with another student. Encourage them to describe their home using simple adjectives and action verbs. For example, *This is the kitchen. It's small. We cook there.*

Choosing Furniture

- Teach basic furniture vocabulary using *The Addison-Wesley Picture Dictionary* or another picture dictionary. Encourage children to ask questions about any words they are not familiar with.

- Give students old magazines with pictures of furniture in them along with drawing materials. Invite them to either draw or cut out pictures of furniture they like and to paste each one on their floor plan next to the room it would go in. Encourage them to share their furniture choices with a partner. They can practice questions with *where,* and responses with prepositions of place. For example, *Where is the sofa?* (It's in the living room.) *Where is the dresser?* (It's near the bed.)

Activities for Intermediate Level Students

Looking for Rhymes

- Read and discuss the Big Book, *A House Is a House for Me,* by Mary Ann Hoberman, with the class. Ask students to tell all the different types of things that were used as houses by the creatures in the story.

- Ask children to find pairs of rhyming words in the story. Have pairs of students work together for a few minutes. Then invite one pair to list their words on newsprint on the wall. Later, others can add to the list. Here are some of the rhyming pairs: *house/mouse, bug/rug, slug/snug, sheep/sleep,* and *hole/mole.*

This activity also provides an opportunity for students to use prepositions of place, such as on, in, at, to, and into, *in a meaningful context.*

NOTE

- Invite students to copy the list and illustrate some of the words. Then ask them to write short sentences using the words and illustrate them with simple drawings like those below.

A mouse runs into a house.

A bug jumps on a rug.

Daysi Abarca, Age 7

MATERIALS

✓ *shoe boxes (or similar boxes)*
✓ *markers*
✓ *3-by-5-inch cards*

Examining Categories

- Label shoe boxes or other similar boxes with the names of several topics you have covered in the class. Make vocabulary cards for words related to those topics and ask students to sort the words into the correct boxes. For example, you might have four boxes labeled *weather, plants, animals,* and *houses* and vocabulary cards like the ones below. Create categories and word cards for any topic you have covered.

deer	oak	bungalow	rainy
cloudy	igloo	tiger	elephant
poplar	snowy	llama	baobab
neem	hogan	skyscraper	sunny

- Beginning level students can make use of the same category boxes. However, you might want to create a beginners' level card set with pictures to accompany the word clues.
- This activity could be extended by having students sort cards into piles of nouns, verbs, adjectives, and adverbs.

Learning About Shapes

READING

✓ Shapes, Shapes, Shapes
by Tana Hoban

- Read *Shapes, Shapes, Shapes,* by Tana Hoban, to the class. Ask students to name any other shapes they know of.
- Draw the following shapes on the board and ask students to name pieces of furniture or parts of the house that are made in each of these shapes.

rectangle
(door)

_____
_____
_____

cone
(lampshade)

_____
_____
_____

circle
(table)

_____
_____
_____

cube
(clothes dryer)

_____
_____
_____

square
(windowpane)

_____
_____
_____

triangle
(roof gable)

_____
_____
_____

semicircle
(window)

_____
_____
_____

M A T E R I A L S

✓ "Shapes" reproducible master, page 63

- Make a copy of the "Shapes" reproducible master on page 63 and ask students to fill in examples of all the shapes they can find in their homes. Go over the completed charts together in class.

- Some students may mention pieces of furniture that are not familiar to the rest of the class. In Asia, for example, *tatami* mats and other straw floor coverings are considered an important element in furnishing a household. Encourage students to describe to the class the appearance and use of any household items which may be unfamiliar to others.

Activities for Advanced Level Students

Using a Web to Generate Vocabulary

- Start with the word *house* and ask students to help you create a web of house words. Show them how to build several

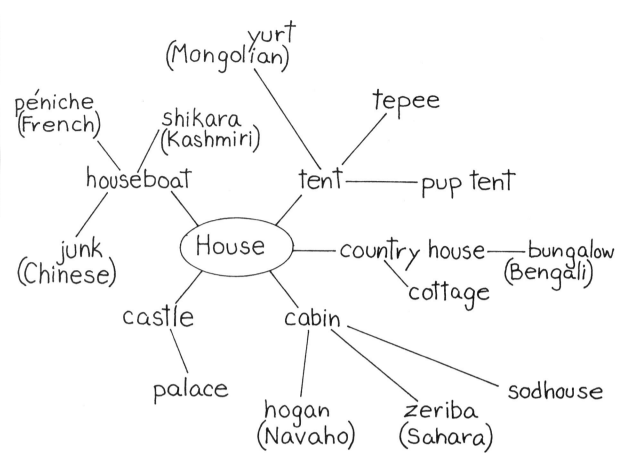

A Sample Web on Houses

supplementary ideas from each secondary idea. Have students explain to others in the class any new words they add, using drawings if necessary. See the sample web above.

- You can combine webbing with research. Ask some students to locate a specific country on the world map and describe the types of houses found there. They can find information in encyclopedias or in books like Carol Bowyer's *The Children's Book of Houses and Homes.*

✓ The Children's Book of
Houses and Homes, *by*
Carol Bowyer.

R
E
A
D
I
N
G

Using Drawings to Record a Brainstorming Activity. A good way to record the words students brainstorm is through the use of a memorable visual format. For example, you might ask them to come up with words that come to mind when they think of home as a place of shelter or refuge. Record their responses in an interesting way, such as on the blocks of an igloo as pictured on the next page.

A Word Igloo

Making a List of Opposites

● Write several adjectives used to describe houses on the board and ask students to give opposites for each one. Then encourage them to add to the list of adjectives and their opposites. Suggest that they copy the list into their notebooks for later reference. Possible pairs include: *light/dark, occupied/vacant,* and *dirty/clean.*

● Make copies of "Josué's High-Rise Apartment" on page 64 and ask students to fill in the list of opposites using the word bank at the bottom of the page. Go over the completed pages together in class.

Brainstorming Professions. Brainstorm a list of the different professions involved in designing and building houses. Students could then expand on this topic and do research as a special project when they get to the Creating and Sharing section.

Exploring the Verbs Make *and* Do

● The verbs *make* and *do* are not interchangeable. Teach students some of the common usages that relate to household activities. Start one of the following lists on the board and ask students to add to it. Suggest that they keep a copy in their notebooks.

You can:	But you always:
make a bed.	do the dishes.
make a meal.	do the laundry.
make a mess.	do the cleaning.

READING AND REFLECTING

With a good, solid vocabulary foundation and a broad overview of the topic, students will now be able to benefit from subsequent reading and research. One of the goals of this chapter is to enable students to eventually understand the concept of the world as a global village.

Activities for All Levels

Using Stories to Learn More About Houses

✓ The Mitten, *by Jan Brett*

READING

- Read *The Mitten,* by Jan Brett, which vividly recreates the snowy landscape surrounding a Ukrainian *dacha* (country house) along with the cozy atmosphere inside. The book provides revealing glimpses into the life of this peaceful rural area. Ask students to list the visual details that the author uses. Then, guide them into drawing a parallel between the solid thatch-roofed dacha, blending in the snowy landscape, and the white mitten lying in the snow, which makes a soft, warm burrow for the mole.

✓ The Little Clay House, *by Elizabeth Cooper*

READING

- Read *The Little Clay House,* by Elizabeth Cooper. This is a Russian folktale about a man who lost a clay jar on his way to the city. Both the mitten and the clay jar become cozy homes for animals. (This ties in well with the chapter on animals in Volume 1 and could lead into a research or enrichment project on animal homes later on.)

- After reading the two books, ask students questions like these about human shelters: *What materials do human beings use to build homes?* (wood, stone, plastic) *Where do these materials come from?* (trees, the earth, factories) *Name some permanent shelters.* (cabins, apartment buildings) *Name some temporary shelters.* (tents, trailers) *Name some groups of people who live in temporary shelters.* (Bedouins in the Sahara, people whose houses have burned down).

Using Charts to Organize Information

- One convenient way to organize the wealth of data students pick up as they read is to record it together in class on comparative charts. These graphic organizers provide a solid framework for categorizing information. They can be displayed throughout the entire unit and referred to by students as often as necessary. The sample comparative chart on page 52 is based on five books about houses.

- This sample chart provides examples of data found in some read-aloud books. As usual, you can use whatever books are available to you for this activity. Remember that students find information in both the written word and the illustrations. The process of filling in the chart helps students see the correlation between architecture, materials used, geography, weather, and natural resources.

Using the My World Series

- This series of attractively illustrated books can be used with all proficiency levels. Ask students to show what they are learning from these books by creating a bulletin board display. Place a world map on the bulletin board. Invite students to draw pictures of the houses they learn about on 3-by-5-inch cards and tack them to the bulletin board. Then ask them to use yarn and pushpins to connect each picture to the appropriate country.

- Invite more advanced students to write an advertisement, like the one below, for each house on another 3-by-5-inch card. Place an ad under each drawing.

READING

✓ A Visit to the Philippines, My Home in Bangladesh, My Home in Brazil, *and* My Home in the Philippines, *all by Donna Bailey and Anna Sproule*

MATERIALS

✓ world map
✓ 3-by-5-inch cards
✓ crayons or markers
✓ pushpins
✓ yarn

KENYA

Beautiful round house
Thatched roof
Walls decorated with patterns
On the shores of Lake Baringo
Abundant fishing and wildlife

TITLE	AUTHOR	LOCATION	GEOGRAPHY & WEATHER	TYPE OF HOUSE	BUILDING MATERIALS & FURNISHINGS
The Village of Round and Square Houses	Ann Grifalconi	The Cameroons (West Africa)	mountainous rich soil hot climate	round houses for women square houses for men	thatched roof stools
Dakota Dugout	Ann Turner	the prairies of the U.S.A.	cold, snowy winters hot, dry summers	sod house or "dugout" (cave)	sod strips cut into bricks buffalo hide door grass on floor
The Golden Tombo	H. Tom Hall	a small farm in Japan	warm Summer	Small farmhouse with a thatched roof	thatched roof paper walls roll-up bed put on shelf
Springtime in Noisy Village	Astrid Lindgren	a village with only 3 farms in Sweden	fields and pastures wet, muddy springs	farmhouses with 2 chimneys woodshed barn playhouse	wood tile roofs flower beds flower pots maypole
The Indian and His Pueblo	Louise Lee Floethe	near the Rio Grande in New Mexico	mesa mountains in distance very dry climate	adobe house flat roof small, high windows	clay + sand made into bricks plastered with more adobe

A Comparative Literature chart

Reading About American Houses

● For a change of pace, you might wish to read *Victoria House,* by Janice Shefelman, about a rural Victorian home which is moved to a street corner in the city and then lovingly restored. Invite students to work together in groups to research and answer these questions: *Why is the house called "Victoria House?" What things make a house a Victorian house? In what years were most Victorian houses built?* Encourage students to bring in pictures of Victorian houses and post them on the bulletin board.

● *Mrs. Tortino's Return to the Sun,* by Shirley and Pat Murphy, is about another old Victorian house. This house was originally built in the middle of the city. However, it gets moved up to the 30th floor of a skyscraper, where the sun always shines and the hustle and bustle of the city can be forgotten. Ask students to compare and contrast the events in this story with those in the previous one. Then ask them what reasons the owners had for moving the houses.

Activities for Advanced Level Students

Using the If You Lived... Series.

● The *If You Lived...* books are written from the point of view of young children, provide useful facts, and are an excellent supplement to the information found in social studies books.

● Review the use of comparative charts (page 51) and ask students to create one which compares these two books with several others on the same topic of living in other places and times.

● Show students how to begin organizing information for a composition about housing in a particular place and time. Hand out 3-by-5-inch index cards and suggest that students make up a note card for each fact they learn from a book and each fact they already know. Then have them sort the piles of cards by topic. Each pile of cards becomes the basis for a paragraph of the composition.

Doing Collaborative Research. Students in the upper elementary grades study a variety of historical periods. Ask a group of children to choose a specific historical period, check out books

✓ Homes and Cities, *by Colin Moorcraft*
✓ Putting the Sun to Work, *by Jeanne Bendick*

R E A D I N G

✓ *chart paper*
✓ *markers*
✓ *reference and history books*

M A T E R I A L S

✓ A Home, *by Lennart Rudström*

R E A D I N G

from the school or public library, and prepare a report. *Homes and Cities,* by Colin Moorcraft, and *Putting the Sun to Work,* by Jeanne Bendick, will be of particular interest to children who are concerned about our dwindling natural resources and the future of the planet.

Making a Timeline. Ask some students to research and draw a timeline showing the types of shelters that have existed since prehistoric times. Suggest that they start with caves and continue on through "smart houses" of the future which are run completely by computers. Help students subtract the dates of past occurrences from today's date to see how many years ago each type of shelter was used. Point out the contributions each cultural group has made to our global heritage. (See instructions for how to construct a timeline on page 27.) Less advanced students can draw pictures while others write in the dates.

Reading for Enjoyment

● Share *A Home,* with paintings by Carl Larsson and a text by Lennart Rudström, with the class. The book depicts a lifestyle now gone. It features a Swedish country home inhabited by a lively, talented family. The watercolor illustrations are full of detail—the beautiful tile ovens, light flooding in through wide windows, potted plants and flowers everywhere. All these details and touches turn this country house into a home.

● Ask students to work in pairs or small groups and list the details of Swedish home life included in Carl Larssons' artwork for the book. Then ask the pairs or groups to share their discoveries with the class. Record all items on chart paper and post it so that students can use it for a later writing assignment.

CREATING AND SHARING

The topic of houses is one which all students get excited about, regardless of where they come from or how old they are. The things they have read about in this chapter provide only part of the background for the creative projects outlined here. Just as important and inspirational are their memories of the past and their hopes for the future.

Activities for Beginning and Intermediate Level Students

Making Castles and Club Houses

● After reading *Christina Katerina and the Box,* by Patricia Lee Gauch, bring two large cardboard boxes to school. Divide students into two groups. Ask one to turn their box into a castle, complete with turrets and a moat. Ask the other group to make their box into a club house.

● Invite students to write about their collaborative work and to share what they have written with others. The cardboard castle and club house could then be used to decorate the Reading Corner.

Learning About Round and Square Houses

● Ask students to read *The Village of Round and Square Houses,* by Ann Grifalconi. Make copies of "The Village of Round and Square Houses" on page 65 and ask students to fill in the blanks and go over their answers with a partner. Later review the responses in class and answer any questions students may have.

MATERIALS

✓ *"The Village of Round and Square Houses" reproducible master, page 65*
✓ *construction paper*
✓ *transparent tape*
✓ *scissors*
✓ *markers or crayons*

● Invite students to create models of the houses in the stories. Hand out pieces of light brown or tan construction paper and other materials and have them use the drawings in the book as a guide. Encourage students to use crayons or markers to add details. To provide an opportunity for students to work in cooperative groups, suggest that each person work with a partner, discussing what they are going to do next, and stopping to answer each other's questions.

Making a Model Community

● After reading *Katy and the Big Snow,* by Virginia Lee Burton, discuss the importance of each job in the community and make a list of some of the buildings mentioned in the story. Discuss their functions and brainstorm for adequate symbols to represent them.

● Ask students to each choose a building and make a small model of it using recycled materials.

● Provide a large piece of white posterboard and assign two students to draw a large map of the city of Geopolis, as it

✓ recycled paper
✓ posterboard
✓ small, red, toy tractor

appears in the book. Then invite students to locate the buildings they have made on the map.

- If possible, bring in a small red toy tractor and invite students to retrace Katy's snow-plowing feat. Writing about the experience will prove to be easy for your students once you have excited and motivated them with these activities.

Making Something from Nothing

✓ Megan Gets a Dollhouse, by Nancy McArthur

- *Megan Gets a Dollhouse,* by Nancy McArthur, is another book which lends itself well to a construction project—doll houses built entirely out of "junk."

- ESL students often enjoy sharing work on a project like this with mainstream students from another class. First they read the book, discuss it in class, and write in their journals. Then they join with members of another class (perhaps a grade up from them) and build their dollhouses together. The final products can be displayed in a showcase near the entrance of the school.

✓ student journals
✓ scraps of paper
✓ small boxes
✓ wallpaper and cloth samples
✓ wooden spools

Activities for Advanced Level Students

Making Dioramas. As a follow-up activity to reading *Little House in the Big Woods* or *Little House on the Prairie,* by Laura Ingalls Wilder, ask students to either draw or build a model of Laura's "little house," following her description as closely as possible. If students choose to build a model, show them how to make the walls stand up by anchoring them to a "floor" of construction paper using transparent tape. Suggest that they cut out various pieces of furniture, color them in, and also attach them to the floor with tape.

✓ Little House in the Big Woods or Little House on the Prairie, by Laura Ingalls Wilder

Making Murals. After reading *Sarah, Plain and Tall,* by Patricia MacLachlan, divide the class into two groups. Have one group draw a mural of Sarah's Maine, complete with a lighthouse, the sea, and the flowers. The other group can divide up the remaining tasks: some students can draw characters; others can do animals; still others can fill in backgrounds and buildings. Putting the mural together involves drawing a map showing how Sarah got to her new home. This activity allows students to learn to work collaboratively, with some doing research while others complete drawings.

✓ Sarah, Plain and Tall, by Patricia MacLachlan

Designing Dream Houses. Ask students to design their ideal homes. They can draw pictures of the outside and inside, and make floor plans if they wish. Suggest that students share their designs with a partner.

Writing Activities for All Levels

Remembering My House in My Country

- Before assigning the writing projects, emphasize to the class that you will be looking at contrasts in building materials, furnishings, and decoration, and that the size or cost of the house is not important. In addition, some students may have been homeless at times. You may want to mention, and perhaps discuss, this painful issue and what we can do to help the homeless in our country.

- Ask beginning level students to write a few sentences to accompany pictures they draw of their former residences. Suggest that they ask their families to help them remember as much as possible. They can also make use of the chart of details from Lennart Rudström's book, *A Home,* that they contributed to earlier in this chapter. (See page 54.)

- Help intermediate and advanced level students learn something about making an outline. Put the following guide on the board and move about the room offering encouragement and answering questions as students organize information about the houses they used to live in.

  1. Topic sentence
  2. Outside
     - Location (city, suburbs, country, etc.)
     - Surroundings (trees, fence, block, etc.)
     - Building materials (walls, roof, etc.)
     - Style (modern, Spanish, colonial, etc.)
  3. Inside
     - Rooms (names, number, layout, etc.)
     - Furniture (color, size, location, etc.)
     - Decorative elements (especially family treasures)
  4. Concluding sentence
     - What things make this house special?

MATERIALS

✓ "House Book Cover" reproducible master, page 66
✓ crayons or markers
✓ composition paper
✓ stapler or hole punch and yarn

MATERIALS

✓ word-processing equipment (if available)

- When they have finished, suggest that students use the outline to write a paragraph about their former homes. Use the paragraph as the basis for a house picture book. Make copies of the "House Book Cover" on page 66 and give one to each student. Providing an interesting cover format for their books can be a powerful motivator for student writing. Suggest that they add color pictures to the cover and interior pages. They can staple the cover and pages together or use a hole punch and yarn.

Writing a Newsletter. Help students put together a newsletter to share with other classes. Assign recorders to gather information about student reactions to stories you have read in class, or any other housing-related topic they wish to talk about. Encourage every child to contribute an item, however small it may be. Collect the stories and enter them into a computer word processor, if possible. Print copies for each student and post a copy on the classroom wall. (See *The Global Classroom*, Volume 1, page 38, for more complete instructions.)

GETTING FAMILIES INVOLVED

As students interview family members to write their *My House in My Country* stories, they can also ask them about some of the customs and traditions observed in their society. For instance, on what occasions did people clean their houses thoroughly? In many western countries, spring cleaning is the one time of the year when the house is cleaned from top to bottom. In Vietnam, however, this happens before Têt (the Lunar New Year), and in China, houses are not only cleaned but also painted to celebrate the New Year.

In the United States people commonly wear shoes at home. In many other countries, people take off their shoes before entering the house. In some places they cover their feet with slippers (France). In others, they go barefoot (Laos, Thailand, India) or wear socks (Japan).

You will have to use your own judgement in discussing religious objects found in the home. The Chinese altar, the Vietnamese ancestor shrine, and the *puja* room found in some

Indian homes are all important household elements. Create an atmosphere of respect for diversity and tolerance of differences when talking about these sacred articles.

A hands-on project that involves both students and families is the making of a model house like those in their native country. I have seen a student who was very resistant to reading and spelling come into his own when he presented the *chalet* he had built for this project. He suddenly found the language he needed to explain the reason for the slanted roof, why slate was used, and much more. Another student spent hours with his father reconstructing a corner of Quito, Ecuador on a sheet of masonite board. They used infinitely thin strips of masking tape to represent the highway lanes. A crumpled brown paper bag, on which artificial moss had been glued, served as the hill behind the high-rise apartments.

These are some of the ways in which you can get your students to tap into their creative powers and at the same time draw family members into the process. Activities such as these help motivate students to learn more, and help get family members involved in the process of learning English.

CONCLUSION

This unit provides a reinforcement of some of the skills presented in the previous chapters, including collecting data, categorizing information, webbing, and developing vocabulary. In addition, it extends the examination of multicultural lifestyles and motivates students to make positive use of their memories of what life was like in their native countries.

SUGGESTED READINGS

(Titles mentioned in this chapter are marked with a ◆.)
Addison-Wesley Publishing Company. The Addison-Wesley Picture Dictionary. Reading, MA: 1984.
◆ Bailey, Donna and Sproule, Anna. *A Visit to the Philippines.* Austin, Texas: Steck-Vaughn, 1991.

♦ ———. *My Home in Bangladesh.* Austin, Texas: Steck-Vaughn, 1991.

♦ ———. *My Home in Brazil.* Austin, Texas: Steck-Vaughn, 1991.

♦ ———. *My Home in the Philippines.* Austin, Texas: Steck-Vaughn, 1991.

♦ Bendick, Jeanne. *Putting the Sun to Work.* Champaign, Illinois: Garrard Publishing Company, 1979.

♦ Bowyer, Carol. *The Children's Book of Houses and Homes.* London: Usborne Publishing, Ltd., 1978.

♦ Brett, Jan. *The Mitten.* New York: G.B. Putnam's Sons, 1989.

Buchanan, Ken. *This House is Made of Mud.* Flagstaff, Arizona: Northland Publishing Company, 1991.

♦ Burton, Virginia Lee. *Katy and the Big Snow.* New York: Scholastic, 1971.

———. *The Little House.* Boston: Houghton Mifflin, 1969.

Clinton, Susan. *I Can Be An Architect.* Chicago: Children's Press, 1986.

Cooney, Barbara. *Hattie and the Wild Waves.* New York: Scholastic, l990.

Cooper, Elizabeth K. *The House on the Hill.* New York: Harcourt Brace Jovanovich, 1976.

♦ ———. *The Little Clay House* (pages 97-101 in *Together We Go*). New York: Harcourt Brace Javanovich, 1970.

Dalgliesh, Alice. *The Silver Pencil.* New York: Puffin Books, 1991.

♦ De Paola, Tomie. *Giorgio's Village.* New York: G.B. Putnam's Sons, 1982.

Edom, Helen. *How Things Are Built.* Tulsa, Oklahoma: EDC Publishers, 1989.

♦ Floethe, Louise Lee. *The Indian and His Pueblo.* New York: Charles Scribner's Sons, 1960.

Fradin, Dennis B. *Space Colonies.* Chicago: Children's Press, 1985.

♦ Gauch, Patricia Lee. *Christina Katerina and the Box.* New York: Putnam Publishing Group, 1980.

Gidal, Sonia and Tim. *My Village in Korea.* New York: Pantheon, 1968.

Goor, Ron and Nancy. Pompeii, *Exploring a Roman Ghost Town.* New York: Thomas Y. Crowell, 1986.

◆ Grifalconi, Ann. *The Village of Round and Square Houses.* Boston: Little, Brown and Company, 1986.

◆ Hall, Tom. *The Golden Tombo.* New York: Alfred A. Knopf, 1959.

◆ Hoban, Tana. *Shapes, Shapes, Shapes.* New York: Greenwillow Books, 1986.

◆ Hoberman, Mary Ann. *A House Is a House for Me.* New York: Viking, 1978.

◆ Lindgren, Astrid. *Springtime in Noisy Village.* New York: Viking Kestrel, 1965.

◆ MacLachlan, Patricia. *Sarah, Plain and Tall.* New York: Harper & Row, 1985.

◆ McArthur, Nancy, *Megan Gets a Dollhouse.* New York, Scholastic, 1988.

◆ McGovern, Ann. *If You Lived in Colonial Times.* New York: Scholastic, 1992.

◆ ————. *If You Lived with the Sioux Indians.* New York: Scholastic, 1992.

◆ Moorcraft, Colin. *Homes and Cities.* New York: Franklin Watts, 1982.

◆ Murphy, Shirley and Pat. *Mrs. Tortino's Return to the Sun.* New York: Lothrop, Lee and Shepard Books, 1980.

Musgrove, Margaret. Ashanti to Zulu. New York: Dial Books for Young Readers, 1980.

Nash, Veronica. *Carlito's World—A Block in Spanish Harlem.* New York: McGraw Hill, 1969.

Nielsen, Virginia. *The House on the Volcano.* New York: Scholastic, 1966.

◆ Patrick, Denise. *Look Inside a House.* New York: Grosset and Dunlap, 1989.

Provensen, Alice and Martin. *Town and Country.* New York: Crown Publishers, 1984.

Robbins, Ken. *Building a House.* New York: Macmillan Publishing Company, 1984.

◆ Rudström, Lennart, with paintings by Carl Larsson. *A Home.* New York, G. B. Putnam's Sons, 1974.

◆ Shefelman, Janice. *Victoria House*. San Diego: Harcourt Brace Jovanovich, 1988.

Stanley, Diane. *Fortune*. New York: Morrow Junior Books, 1990.

Tresselt, Alvin. *Wake Up, City*. New York: Lothrop, Lee and Shepard, 1957.

◆ Turner, Ann. *Dakota Dugout*. New York: Macmillan Publishing Company, 1985.

———. *Heron Street*. New York: Scholastic, 1991.

◆ Wilder, Laura Ingalls. *Little House in the Big Woods*. New York: Harper & Row, 1971.

◆ ———. *Little House on the Prairie*. New York: Harper & Row, 1971.

◆ Wilson, Forrest. *What It Feels Like to Be a Building*. Washington, D.C.: The Preservation Press, 1988.

ADDITIONAL RESOURCES

Smallwood, Betty Ansin. *The Literature Connection: A Read-Aloud Guide for Multicultural Classrooms*. Reading, MA: Addison-Wesley, 1991. (This annotated guide to multicultural literature lists additional titles in its section on House/Home, pages 76–79.)

SHAPES

Name_____ Date _____

See how many items in your house you can list under each shape category.

Circle	Square	Triangle
stool		

Rectangle	Cylinder	Cube

JOSUÉ'S HIGH-RISE APARTMENT

Name_____ Date _____

Please help Josué match the words on the ten floors of his apartment building with the words from the word bank.

burrow

cozy

dilapidated

housing

landlord

roomy

spotless

squalid

tenant

vacant

Word Bank

comfortable	den	dirty	dwelling	empty
immaculate	owner	renter	rickety	spacious

THE VILLAGE OF ROUND AND SQUARE HOUSES

Name_____ Date _____

Complete the sentences with words from the word bank.

A long time ago, in a small village in Africa, a _____

erupted and everything was covered with _____. Now the

_____ is very rich. Coffee and cassava are two of the

main _____. In this village, women still live in

_____ houses and men live in _____ houses.

All the houses have _____ roofs. At dinner time, the

grandfather sits on the highest _____ and eats first, because

he is the _____. The youngest child carries hot water and

they all wash their hands before dinner. The children's favorite food is

_____, which is made from cassava.

ash

crops   fou-fou

oldest   round   soil

square   stool   thatched   volcano

65

Copyright 1995 Addison-Wesley Publishing Company

HOUSE BOOK COVER

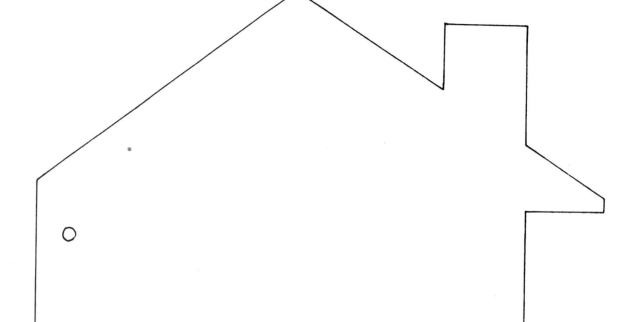

(Circles are a hole punch guide.)

TRANSPORTATION ALTERNATIVES

Chapter

3

FROM CAMEL TO JET

CONTENT AREA LEARNING WEB

TRANSPORTATION ALTERNATIVES

CHAPTER 3. TRANSPORTATION ALTERNATIVES

Poner el carro delante de las mulas.

Don't put the cart before the horse.

—SPANISH PROVERB

This chapter offers a variety of topics and strategies which can be introduced at any time during the year. It presents many opportunities for students to discuss how people and goods are transported in their countries of origin and in the United States. They will have a chance to compare and contrast transportation systems in a variety of geographical locations and historical time periods. As you make long-range plans, you should plan to allow two to three weeks to cover each of the major subtopics in this chapter—exploration and aviation.

You might try to schedule the material on exploration, with an emphasis on Hispanic explorers, to coincide with Hispanic Heritage Month (September 15 through October 15). Otherwise, you could review the social studies curriculum and try to coordinate the presentation of this unit with related material that appears in that program.

The aviation section provides a variety of hands-on activities and helps students integrate some of the knowledge they have gained and the skills they have been developing throughout the year. It includes work on vocabulary, reading, social studies, mathematics, and science, and also activates students' artistic skills. Students at all proficiency levels will be able to participate fully. This section culminates with the creation of a large-scale model of an airliner which serves as a stage set and is shared with the whole school.

SPARKING INTEREST

A great deal of information about transportation is readily available no matter where you live. Most printed material is accompanied by colorful photographs and illustrations, and travel brochures and posters are always free. Students can begin by sharing their own travel experiences and move on to a more general discussion of modes of transportation.

✓ posters and
advertisements
✓ back issues of the
National Geographic
magazine

Garage sales are a good
source of magazines and
realia. Introduce yourself as
a teacher and offer to pick
up unsold items at the end
of the day.

✓ television or video
playback equipment and
videotape of a space
shuttle launch

✓ book of nursery rhymes

Using Visual Stimuli

- Create an Art Corner where students can put up posters, calendars, and pictures from the travel section of the newspaper. Encourage groups of children to gather there and discuss what they see.

- Use pictures from back issues of the *National Geographic* magazine to transport students to a faraway place. Take them on a barge trip down a canal in Burgundy or on a balloon ride over the Sahara desert. Hold up the pages so that all students can see clearly as you briefly explain what is going on in each picture and elicit comments and questions.

- These same pictures can be brought out again later and used as the focus of a writing assignment. Although the language level of the magazine may be too high, students may be able to find key words in the text for use in their own compositions.

- Set up a display of books, photographs, and scale models featuring modes of transportation. Try to include a wide variety of vehicles, including oxcarts, tongas, canoes, covered wagons, sleds, jet planes, bicycles, and hot air balloons. Encourage students to bring in pictures or models from home to add to the collection.

- Watch the launch of a space shuttle. If one is taking place during school hours, try to watch it live. Otherwise, show a videotape of a launch. Before watching the tape, ask students to predict what will happen and hold a mock countdown.

- Share an album of photographs depicting a trip you have taken or a country you have visited.

- Invite students to close their eyes and mentally retrace a trip from home to school, or the journey from their country of origin to their current home. Suggest that they try to visualize the various things they saw along the way.

Using Auditory Stimuli

- Teach students some nursery rhymes which feature transportation, such as *Ride a Cock Horse to Banbury Cross* or *The Owl and the Pussycat*.

- Ask students to share similar nursery rhymes or childhood ditties from their countries of origin. First have them present the rhyme in the original language. Then have them tell what it is about and provide a rough translation.

- Play recordings of transportation-related songs, such as "Over the River and Through the Woods" (traditional), "Yellow Submarine" by the Beatles, and "Country Roads," by John Denver (or others of your choice). Help students pick out words and phrases relating to transportation. Provide written lyrics for intermediate and advanced students. If students are interested, teach them to sing one of the songs.

- Invite students to imitate the sounds made by various modes of transportation. These sounds may include an ambulance siren, a traffic helicopter, an ocean liner coming into port, a snowplow, a lawn mower, a fire truck, and a supersonic jet.

READING

✓ *The Little Engine That Could, by Watty Piper*
✓ *Not So Fast, Songololo, by Niki Daly*
✓ *Ox-Cart Man, by Donald Hall*

- Read aloud some of these books: *The Little Engine That Could; Not So Fast, Songololo; Ox-Cart Man.* Invite children to point out words that describe motion. Ask them to repeat any phrases that catch their ears. Then encourage them to join in on these phrases as you read the story a second time.

Using Kinesthetic Stimuli

Pantomime riding a bicycle, boarding a bus, riding a burro, riding a camel, sailing a boat, flying an airplane, or taking a trip on a train. Ask students to guess what you are doing in each case. Then invite the student who correctly identifies your last pantomime to do one for the rest of the class to guess. Continue the activity by having each person who guesses correctly perform another one.

EXPANDING LANGUAGE

Now that you have raised the level of interest in the topic, it's time to develop students' language through the use of charts, webs, and other classroom activities. The varied backgrounds of your students are a valuable asset since various students will be able to describe different modes of transport and tell about different types of travel experiences.

To begin this part of the chapter, start out by making a list of all the ways students might get themselves to school every day—by bus, bike, car, or on foot. Some may be accompanied by younger siblings in baby carriages or strollers. Mention people who may be involved in the journey such as the bus driver, the crossing guard, or a friend's mother. Ask what other types of transportation they might see on the way to school (a police car, a fire truck, a jet plane, or possibly even a tugboat). Later, ask students to visualize the trip they made from home to school in their native countries. The sharing session which follows will reflect the diversity in your classroom and the multicultural lifestyles of your students. It will also provide you with fresh insights into their lives.

If you wish, you can make a chart showing the means of transportation used by all the students when they left their home countries and moved to the United States. If there is a great variety of answers, ask students to classify the responses into three categories—air, sea, and land.

Activities for Beginning Level Students

Using Charts to Build Vocabulary. Give each student a piece of paper which has been divided into three columns. Write the words *air, land,* and *sea* on the board. Ask students to draw pictures and/or write the names of things that can travel on land, on the water, or in the air. Then elicit verbal responses to some simple questions, such as: *Can a boat go in the air? Can a boat go in water? Can an airplane go in water? Can a bus go on land?* The grammatical difficulties are minimal, since *can* is followed by the simple form of the verb.

Drawing a Picture. Later, inject some questions with *Where* and *What* and practice similar answers. Invite students to choose their favorite way to go someplace, draw a picture, and write a sentence or a short paragraph about it, if they wish. Collect the pictures and post them on the bulletin board.

Activities for Intermediate Level Students

Working with Charts

- Brainstorm with students the categories and subcategories to use when making a master chart of all types of transportation. If you wish, you can start with the categories presented

LAND

Human	Animal	Mechanical
walking	riding a horse	driving a car
riding a bicycle	riding a donkey	taking a train
riding a tricycle	driving an oxcart	riding a motorcycle
riding a rickshaw	driving a dogsled	driving a tractor
using a wheelchair	driving a camel cart	taking a subway
being carried on a litter		taking a bus
riding a sled		taking a cablecar

SEA

Human	Animal	Mechanical
riding a raft	using a barge	taking a ferry
rowing a boat	pulled by a mule	driving a motorboat
sailing a boat		riding a hydrofoil
taking a gondola		taking an oceanliner
paddling a canoe		riding in a submarine

AIR

Human	Animal	Mechanical
riding in a balloon	flying	taking a jet
riding in a glider		taking a helicopter
taking a hanglider ride		going by rocket
flying an ultralight		taking a plane

to beginning level students. Here is an example of what a completed classification chart might look like.

● As you go over the chart, ask students to compare and contrast the means of transportation used in various parts of the world and invite them to locate those places on a map or a globe of the world. Then ask questions like these: *What vehicles do you see along the highways in El Salvador? Are school buses painted yellow in Japan? What special designs are painted on public buses in your native country? Can people ride outside the bus? on top of the bus? Which side of the road do cars drive on? Are distances measured in kilometers or miles?*

Activities for Advanced Level Students

Using Charts to Build Vocabulary

- This may be a good time for students to take a look at a variety of travel terms that are used in different contexts. The examples given in the diagram and lists on page 75 will give you an idea of some of the kinds of charts you can generate with the class. These samples include a number of cognates.

- Strangely enough, many ESL students find it easier to understand polysyllabic words such as *expedition* or *exploration,* than monosyllabic nouns like *trip.* This is because the *ex-* words have Latin roots, while the word *trip* is derived from the Old English *treppan* (to tread) or Middle English *trippen* (to step lightly). Start students out with some of the ideas on each of the diagrams and see how many elements they can add. What other types of diagrams do they want to make?

Using the Prefixes bi- *and* tri-. Explain the importance of knowing prefixes such as *bi-* and *tri-* and explain that many of them come from Latin and Greek roots. Ask students to name some other common prefixes. Then copy the two lists below onto chart paper and see how many other words students can add to each.

bi-	*tri-*
bicycle	triangle
biplane	triceps
bilingual	tricycle
biped	trident

✓ *"Spanish Explorers Vocabulary Quiz" reproducible master, page 94*

MATERIALS

Using the Suffix -tion. Since nouns like *aviation, expedition,* and *exploration* occur so frequently in this chapter, why not make up a vocabulary list out of the most commonly used *tion* words? This list may be used both to build vocabulary and to practice spelling. Sample words include: *aviation, expedition,*

A Travel Web

```
                        pilgrim
      explorer             |
                        pilgrimage            sailor
            explore           |           sail
                                                    
traveller——travel——( TRIP )——flight————flyer
                                                    
          explore            |            tour
                         expedition                
       explorer                              tourist
                    NOT expediter
```

Travel Verbs

on foot	by boat	by air
walk	glide	soar
wander	float	take off
rove	chug along	dive
roam	cruise	land
saunter	sail	zoom
mosey	embark	
run	disembark	
jog		

exploration, information, location, navigation, direction, and *observation.* Make copies of the "Spanish Explorers Vocabulary Quiz" on page 94 and give each student a copy. Go over the answers after they have completed the quiz.

Spelling Words with the Long A Sound. The words *airplane, railway, train,* and *freight* provide an ideal springboard for a mini-lesson on various spellings of the long *a* sound. Here is a

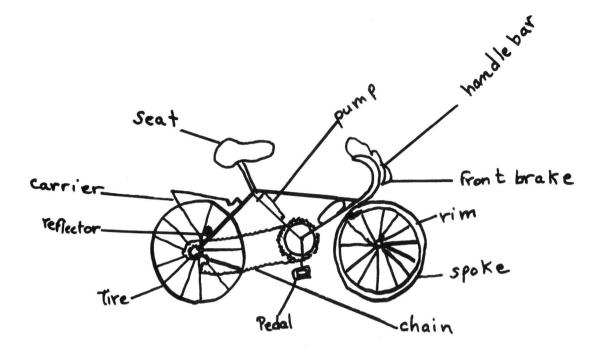

Evelin Abarca, Age 11

partial listing of words using the four different spellings. Put some of these on the board and ask students to add their own words to each list.

a...e	ai	ay	eigh
fare	airplane	bay	eight
gate	railway	stay	freight
brake	trail	runway	weight

Activities for All Levels

Focusing on One Vehicle. Once all this information about transportation has been gathered, ask each student to focus for a few moments on one of the following vehicles: bike, car, train, boat, airplane, or cart. Invite them to draw the vehicle using a picture dictionary or other reference book and label the most important parts. Copy one of the diagrams shown here on the board as an example.

✓ Draw 50 Boats, Ships, Trucks, and Trains, *by Lee J. Ames*

R E A D I N G

Learning to Draw Vehicles. *Draw 50 Boats, Ships, Trucks, and Trains,* by Lee J. Ames, is a tremendous asset to those of us who cannot draw. In six step-by-step sketches, going from a few strokes to a finished picture, the author shows how to draw a Native American paddling a canoe, a moving van, and a train complete with engine and caboose. Add it to your Art Corner for students to use as reference.

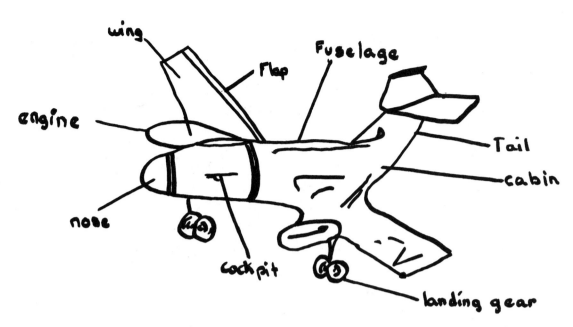

Caleb Anzoleaga, Age 11

Discussing Safety Issues. As you discuss the various means of transportation, take time out to talk about safety rules associated with each one. Emphasize the importance of wearing a bicycle helmet, reasons for fastening the seatbelt when riding in a car, etc.

Improving Pronunciation. Some ESL students have difficulty differentiating between minimal pairs with short and long vowel sound differences. Spanish and French speakers may benefit from practice with pairs such as *ship/sheep.* Others, particularly Asian students, can use extra help with final *t* and *d* sounds as in the *cart/card* pair. Do an oral minimal pair activity in class. Say pairs of words and ask students to say *same* if they think you have said the same word twice (*ship/ship*), and *different* if the two words do not sound exactly the same (*ship/sheep*). As you continue to play the game, students' ability to hear the differences will gradually improve.

READING AND REFLECTING

As you think about the reading activities you want to use for this chapter, don't forget to include the services of the librarian and the reading teacher. With their assistance, students will be able to select books matched to their reading levels. Some students may be able to visit a regional library and discover new titles to add to the list.

Activities for All Levels

Traveling on Water. *Boats,* by Ken Robbins, features photographs of various types of boats, from canoe to submarine. Each photo is accompanied by a short, simple description of the type of boat shown in the picture. Invite students to choose one of the boats and write a paragraph about it in their notebooks. Suggest that they choose one they are somewhat familiar with. Point out elements that make for a good informative writing, such as a clear topic sentence and the use of simple, descriptive adjectives.

Traveling During Bad Weather

- Another book which appeals to young readers is *Snow Day,* by Betsy Maestro. A simple explanation accompanies each detailed illustration. These pictures are based on photographs of actual snow-removal equipment. As they read the book, students become aware of the theme of interdependence which is central to *The Global Classroom.* Before normal transportation can resume, roads must be cleared, and tow trucks, snow plows, and tank trucks must perform their important tasks.

- Ask students to think about how a flood affects transportation. Invite them to work in small groups and draw webs using whatever ideas they come up with. Then combine elements from the various webs into a large web on chart paper. Invite children to write something about how floods affect transportation using this master web as a resource.

Riding a Camel. Ask students to compare and contrast the books *Abdul,* by Rosemary Wells, and *Camels, Ships of the Desert,* by John F. Waters. This activity provides a good opportunity to reinforce the difference between fiction and nonfiction. Ask questions like these: *Which book gives more factual information about camels? Which book contains scientific information? Which book makes you feel happy and sad? Which story has a moral? In your own words, what is the difference between fiction and nonfiction?*

✓ Boats, *by Ken Robbins* — **READING**

✓ Snow Day, *by Betsy Maestro* — **READING**

✓ Abdul, *by Rosemary Wells*
✓ Camels, Ships of the Desert, *by John F. Waters* — **READING**

Using Animals for Transportation

- Introduce students to the true story of Balto, the sled-dog who carried medicine to the sick children of Nome, Alaska, despite a raging blizzard, in *The Bravest Dog Ever,* by Natalie Standiford. Encourage more advanced students to do some research on Alaskan Malamutes or Siberian Huskies and present their findings to the rest of the class.

- If possible, invite someone to bring an Alaskan Malamute or a Siberian Husky to school. Help the class prepare questions to ask the owner before the visit.

- Read *Candido,* by Alberta Eiseman, and discuss the illustrations with students. Draw students' attention to the mountainous terrain, steep trails, and treacherous rope bridges that the llamas cross to bring food and other essentials to the Andean people.

- Brainstorm a list of animals that are used to transport goods and people around the world. This list includes burros, camels, donkeys, elephants, llamas, water buffalo, and yaks. Help students identify countries where each animal is commonly found.

- Read one of the books in the "Vanishing Cultures" series, such as *Himalaya* or *Sahara,* both by Jan Reynolds. Ask students to contrast the kind of information they found in *Candido* with the information in the Reynolds books. Ask: *Which books are fiction and which are nonfiction? How do you know? Why are such books important? What other vanishing cultures do you know of?*

Meeting a Special Train

- *The Little Engine That Could,* by Watty Piper, is another big hit with young readers. Try reading it in three installments. Build up the suspense and celebrate the happy ending.

- Read *The Little Engine That Could* a second time, asking students to raise their hands when they hear a word or phrase that tells how the train moves. For example: "...ran along the track," "...came to a stop," and "...her wheels just would not turn." Encourage students to act out the movement they are describing. At the end of each description ask the student to retell what has happened so far, and predict what will happen next.

✓ My Home in Bangladesh, River Life in Bangladesh, *and* A Visit to the Philippines, *all by Donna Bailey and Anna Sproule*

R E A D I N G

Reading about Flying. In *Abuela,* by Arthur Dorros, the author shows the reader what it feels like to fly, describing an imaginary flight during which a little girl and her grandmother fly over New York and pick out several famous landmarks. Ask students to compare the flight in the book with flights they may have taken. Then ask them what the landmarks in your area would be and how they would look from the air. Invite children to draw pictures of their neighborhood as seen from the air.

Learning about Unusual Vehicles

- *My Home in Bangladesh,* by Donna Bailey and Anna Sproule, pictures the importance of the rickshaw as a means of transportation and as a livelihood for many people in the busy capital city of Dacca.

- In *River Life in Bangladesh,* the same authors effectively portray the role played by boats in providing transportation, both for workers and for cargo.

- In *A Visit to the Philippines,* the same authors use photographs to show tourists travelling by "jeepney" to Manila, while a Filipino farmer rides his buffalo home.

- Ask students to write a response in their journals telling about the various means of transportation they have used in their lives. Ask them to mention any other modes of transport they would like to try and to describe the appeal of each one.

Traveling on Foot

- *Not So Fast, Songololo,* by Niki Daly, is very popular among second and third grade students of all proficiency levels. Students avidly follow young Songololo as he escorts his old Granny to town to do her shopping.

- Invite students to retell the story of how Songololo managed to get Granny across the intersection as seen from the point of view of "the Little Green Man." Record their accounts and use them outside of class to evaluate students' oral skills and as part of a permanent record of their work.

Keeping Records. You can also create "Individual Oral Skills Observation Sheets" for each of your students. On these sheets you can list the different vocabulary development areas that are the focus of your work for the year (greetings, commands, parts of the body, etc.). Under each heading, list specific language items students use to express themselves. Then, on a regular basis, you can track each student's progress as his or her vocabulary develops.

Exploring Egypt

✓ The Day of Ahmed's Secret, *by Florence Parry Heide and Judith Heide Gilliland*

READING

- The bustle, traffic congestion, and noise of a large city are artfully described in *The Day of Ahmed's Secret,* by Florence Parry Heide and Judith Heide Gilliland. In this book, Ahmed, a young Egyptian boy, works very hard to help support his family.

- Ask students to notice how the artist uses light in the illustrations. Point out how the light illuminates Ahmed's face and reveals the curiosity and intelligence in his eyes. It also shines on his hands, in which he holds a pencil and paper. Help students understand why Ahmed's ability to write his own name is so important to him. This might lead to a discussion of how literacy allows people to make a better life for themselves and their families.

Leaving Home

✓ How Many Days to America?, *by Eve Bunting*

READING

- The poignant *How Many Days to America?,* by Eve Bunting, tells of some of the hardships endured by refugees from a Caribbean island who must suddenly leave their village and run for their lives. The story becomes moving and real to students because it is written in the first person and because the illustrations are done from the point of view of the frightened children in the story.

- If possible, discuss this book at Thanksgiving time and ask students to compare it with the story of the Pilgrims coming to America. Some children may wish to compare it to their own experiences escaping dangerous situations. Invite students to write a response in their journals.

✓ Where Is Tibet?, *by Gina Halpern*

READING

- *How Many Days to America?* provides a stark contrast to another book on refugee children, *Where Is Tibet?*, by Gina Halpern. This book features two young Tibetan children, Pema and Tashi, born in exile in India, who ask their families about their homeland, Tibet. Each page has three kinds of writing on it: the Tibetan words, phonetic symbols for each word, and an English translation of the text. This presentation greatly interested my students, who are curious observers of all alphabets.

Writing to an Author. Encourage students who are moved by a particular story to write to the author. Beginning level learners may need to dictate the letters, while more advanced learners can write their own with a little guidance from you. You can write to an author using the publisher's address. Page 83 shows an example of a group letter written to the author of *Where is Tibet?*

Getting Around in the Early Days

✓ If You Lived in Colonial Times, *by Ann McGovern*
READING

- *If You Lived in Colonial Times,* by Ann McGovern, is especially interesting to young students, since it describes the exciting lives of children who lived several hundred years ago. Students learn about different types of sleighs that were used. Some students may be able to compare the narrow roads in the book to trails and paths found in their native countries.

- Ask students to draw and label a three-part picture. Part one can show a mode of transportation used in the story, part two a different means of transport used in their native countries, and part three a vehicle they see every day. If possible, make this a homework assignment so that family members can be involved.

✓ If You Traveled West In a Covered Wagon, *by Ellen Levine*
READING

- *If You Traveled West In a Covered Wagon,* by Ellen Levine, includes an especially useful table of contents containing a list of specific questions to which students will be able to provide answers, once they have read the book.

- After finishing the book, ask students to work in small groups to answer the questions. Then invite each group to share its findings with the rest of the class.

✓ Cassie's Journey, *by Brett Harvey*
✓ My Prairie Year, *by Brett Harvey*
✓ Sacajawea, Wilderness Guide, *by Kate Jassem*
READING

- Other books, such as *Cassie's Journey,* by Brett Harvey, and *My Prairie Year,* based on the diary of Elinore Plaisted, are both informative and realistic and are written in the first person. *Sacajawea, Wilderness Guide,* by Kate Jassem, retraces the life of a Shoshone chief's daughter who grew up in the Rocky Mountains, was sold into slavery, and finally served as a guide for Lewis and Clark as they crossed the Rocky Mountains.

- Encourage students to write about their reactions to one or all of these books in their journals. The response could take the form of several diary entries that might have been made by one of the characters. Another approach would be to have

Ms. De Cou-Landberg
Forest Edge Elementary
1501 Beacontree Lane
Reston, Virginia 22090

Ms. Gina Halpern
c/o Snow Lion Publications
P.O. Box 6483
Ithaca, New York 14850

Dear Ms. Halpern,

We are the students of Ms. Michelle De Cou-Landberg's ESL (English as a Second Language) class. Ms. De Cou-Landberg recently shared your book WHERE IS TIBET? with us and we think your story was wonderful. We talked about how we need to use our minds and our hearts. The story taught us not to believe in fighting. We liked learning about new animals . . . the snow lion, the dragon and the yak.

We all had many comments to make about your book. Here's what we had to say:

CECILIA: I liked the drawing. I might be an author like you. The children's clothes are different from ours.

KASHIF: I liked the pictures in the book. I liked the story. I liked the dragon.

LIEN: I liked the whole book. How did you know how to write in Tibetan?

JULIO: I liked the dragon. He didn't look too frightening!

We also had some questions about you and our story. How did you make the bright colors in the book? Why did the boy wear a dress? What gave you the idea for the designs in your illustrations? How did you make the cover?

Please write back and tell us all about your ideas as you were writing your book, as well as your travels in Tibet.

Sincerely,

Ms. De Cou-Landberg & Second Graders

the students pretend to be one of the characters and make up additional adventures that might have occurred.

CREATING AND SHARING

In this section, you will find activity suggestions geared for students at various proficiency levels. Students will learn about explorers (a special kind of traveler), compare their travel experiences with those of others, and, at the end, create their own jet plane.

Activities for Beginning Level Students

Taking a Second Look

✔ The Little Engine That Could, *by Watty Piper*

R
E
A
D
I
N
G

- Reread *The Little Engine That Could,* by Watty Piper, and give each student a long strip of computer paper folded into three parts. Print the words *beginning, middle,* and *end* on the board, and ask students to copy one of the words at the top of each section. Invite them to draw pictures illustrating these three parts of the book. Ask them to write a few sentences (or single words) about each section of the story. Encourage students to share their work with a partner.

✔ Not So Fast, Songololo, *by Niki Daly*

R
E
A
D
I
N
G

- Reread *Not So Fast, Songololo,* by Niki Daly, and show students how to make their own "tackies" like the ones Songololo's Granny buys him at the end of the story. Have students use recycled paper to trace the outline of one of their shoes. (Demonstrate how to do this by taking off one of your shoes and tracing around it.) Ask students to decorate their "tackies" however they wish. Tape the finished products to the classroom wall. Then ask students to compare and contrast the shoes class members are wearing. Discuss size, color, shape, pattern, and brand. Make a bar graph showing how many students are wearing each type of shoe.

✔ *a world atlas*

M
A
T
E
R
I
A
L
S

Activities for Intermediate and Advanced Level Students

Making Maps. Have students make relief maps of Spanish-speaking countries such as Spain, Mexico, or Colombia. Show

T
R
A N
N S L
S P T
P O E
O R R
R T N
T A A
A T T
T I I
I O V
O N E
N S

them how to interpret the colors on relief maps in an atlas. Then help them use flour and salt dough to make a map of the country on a sheet of corrugated cardboard. When the maps are dry, the colors showing elevations can be painted on. Invite children to share their maps with classmates and to display them in a public place, possibly near the school entrance.

Making Dioramas. Invite students to create dioramas featuring well-know Latina or Latino figures. They might choose someone like Pablo Picasso, Rita Moreno, Roberto Clemente, or Caesar Chavez. Give each student a copy of the "Research Questions" reproducibles on pages 95–96. Enlist the aid of the librarian in helping children research the person they have chosen. Help students choose a scene from the person's life to present in diorama form. Refer back to the instructions for making dioramas on page 56 of this book. Ask children to describe their finished scenes to the class. Keep the scenes on display for several days.

MATERIALS

✓ *"Research Questions" reproducible master, pages 95–96*
✓ *markers*
✓ *construction paper*
✓ *scissors*
✓ *transparent tape*

Dramatizing a Story. Help children prepare and present short scenes from the lives of famous Spanish-speaking explorers. Ask them to work in cooperative groups. Suggest that they use as sources books such as *Meet the Men who Sailed the Seas,* by John Dyment, or *Christopher Columbus,* by Stephen Krensky. Help each group choose a scene and show them how to write out a script using each speaker's name followed by a colon and the words he or she says. Have children present their scenes to the class. Encourage other students to ask questions at the end of the presentations.

READING

✓ Meet the Men who Sailed the Seas, *by John Dyment*
✓ Christopher Columbus, *by Stephen Krensky*

Making a Timeline

- Ask students to create a timeline of aviation history starting with the mythical flight of Icarus in ancient Greece, continuing right up to the latest space probe. (Review the instructions, format, and materials suggested for the clothing timeline on page 27 of this book.)

- Supply the necessary research materials, including encyclopedias, social studies texts, and children's magazines with articles on aviation. Ask each student to research a different event and to draw a picture of it to place on the timeline. Have each person describe his or her contribution and answer questions about it.

- Post the timeline on a classroom wall and refer to it as you

MATERIALS

✓ *computer printouts with one clean side*
✓ *drawing paper*
✓ *markers*
✓ *transparent tape*
✓ *children's encyclopedia*
✓ *social studies textbooks*
✓ *children's magazines with articles on aviation*

continue to teach the unit. Encourage students to add items to it as they read about other exciting events.

Experimenting with Aerodynamics. Encourage students to write to the National Air and Space Museum in Washington, D.C. for free information on air travel. The museum will supply interesting materials on the historical and scientific aspects of flight, along with suggestions for hands-on experiments which students can perform in class. This project includes a writing activity, a highly-motivating reading experience, and the opportunity for language-intensive cooperative activities which are carried out in class where the teacher can provide supervision and language support.

Inventing Board Games. Encourage groups of students to invent their own board games using air travel vocabulary. Brainstorm a master list of terms together. Then ask children to work in small groups. Each square on the board can feature a different vocabulary item followed by an instruction. For example, one square might say, *TAKEOFF—Move six squares forward.* Another might say *FLIGHT DELAYED—Move back two squares.* Children can design their own game pieces in the shape of airplanes and use a spinner or dice to determine how many squares to move. After they have tried out the games, invite students to share theirs with another group.

Making a Life-Size Model

- Invite students to build their own life-size model of a passenger jet in the classroom. This project involves content from the areas of math, science, and social studies. It can start children thinking about possible career choices and can build connections between classroom and community. Ask for input from families, local flight attendants or pilots, the aviation teacher at the local high school (if there is one)—from anyone with bright ideas and building skills.

- The diagram on the following page will give you some idea of how to go about building your model. You can adjust it to fit your own time limits and the availability of materials and construction help.

- Start with some research and reading activities to help students gather any information they need. Discuss what these sources have to say about the physics of flight (gravity, lift,

Side View from Inside

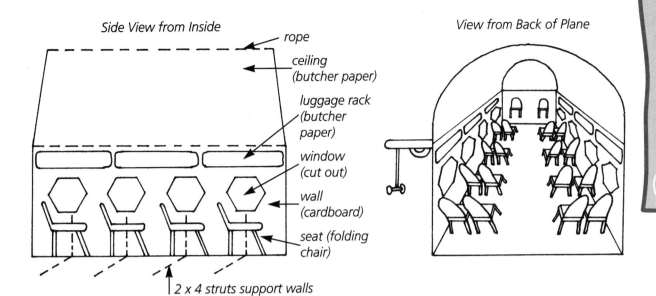

rope

ceiling (butcher paper)

luggage rack (butcher paper)

window (cut out)

wall (cardboard)

seat (folding chair)

2 x 4 struts support walls

View from Back of Plane

Top View

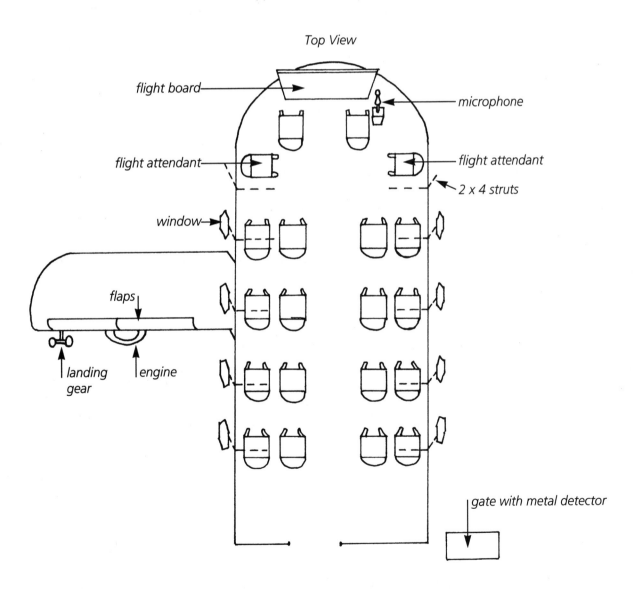

flight board

microphone

flight attendant

flight attendant

2 x 4 struts

window

flaps

landing gear

engine

gate with metal detector

MATERIALS

✓ *items needed to construct the life-size model*

thrust, and drag). This topic provides a perfect connection with the science area.

- Next have students brainstorm how they wish to construct their airplane. Have groups put together floor plans and sketches and help them make a master plan based on the best elements from each. This will involve measuring and mathematical computation as well as artistic expression.

- Gather the materials needed for construction of the plane. This may include cardboard for walls, butcher paper for the ceiling and other surfaces, glue, crayons and markers, scissors to use in designing and attaching details, and other materials, depending on your plans. You can use rope to suspend the ceiling of the airplane, 2 × 4 lumber for wall supports, a telephone cable spool for landing gear, fried chicken buckets for jet engines, and folding chairs for seats. No doubt you will discover many other items that can be used to represent various parts of a plane. This part of the project can lead to involvement by residents of the community as well as family members.

- Elicit help from a shop teacher, family members, or other volunteers to build the 2 × 4 frame.

- Put up and decorate walls and ceiling, cut out the windows, and attach jet engines and other parts of the plane. Place seats in the completed airplane.

MATERIALS

✓ *clothing representing flight crew uniforms*
✓ *homemade badges*
✓ *empty suitcases*

- Invite children to dress in appropriate clothing and role-play a flight. The crew can dress in white shirts and dark pants and wear whatever caps and jackets they can find that resemble flight crew clothing. They can make their own badges. The flight crew should meet together ahead of time to plan their speeches. Passengers can board the plane in family groupings carrying luggage.

- Consider inviting family members and other classes to come to see the plane "take off."

Consider building an ox-cart, a truck, or even the raft, Kon-Tiki. *Whatever the focus, the project will strengthen the bonds between you and your students and will create connections with colleagues.*

NOTE

GETTING FAMILIES INVOLVED

The contributions of family members can help make students' research into modes of transportation used in their native countries a relevant and interesting activity. The cooperation of families is also essential to the success of the airplane-building activity and other class projects.

Students can ask family members about how they got to their present location. In which direction did they travel? How long did the trip take? What modes of transportation did they use?

Children may discuss with their families current modes of transportation in their native country and compare and contrast them with those used by the previous generation. Students may share their findings with the class or write about them in their journals.

The time spent on school projects helps form a strong bond between students and family members. Encourage them to work together to build a model of a canoe, an airplane, an ox-cart, or any other mode of transportation that is of interest to them.

Tap the expertise of family members, possibly in conjunction with a discussion of transportation-related careers. Invite students' relatives to talk to the class about their occupations. Stress the importance of every single job and how it fits into the overall transportation picture.

When studying Spanish explorers and the role played by Christopher Columbus, ask students to talk with their families about these events and to write down family responses in their journal. These reactions may then be shared in class and used as the basis for a discussion of the contributions of various cultures to the growth of the United States.

CONCLUSION

This chapter on transportation helps demonstrate the connections that exist among all aspects of *The Global Classroom*. Llamas appeared in the animals chapter and reappear here since they provide an important mode of transportation for goods on the mountainous trails of the Andes. Weather patterns and seasons (Volume 1, Chapter 1), affect sailing and flying patterns. The activities in this chapter also make us aware of our dependence on others—peers, teachers, family members, friends—who share their time, their knowledge, and their special skills with us.

SUGGESTED READINGS

(Titles mentioned in this chapter are marked with a •.)

♦ Ames, Lee J. *Draw 50 Boats, Ships, Trucks, and Trains.* Garden City, New York: Doubleday & Co., 1976.

Angel, Ann. *John Glenn, Space Pioneer.* New York: Ballantine Books, 1989.

♦ Bailey, Donna and Sproule, Anna. *A Visit to the Philippines.* Austin, Texas: Steck-Vaughn, 1991.

♦ —— *My Home in Bangladesh.* Austin, Texas: Steck-Vaughn, 1991.

♦ —— *River Life in Bangladesh.* Austin, Texas: Steck-Vaughn, 1991.

♦ Bunting, Eve. *How Many Days to America?* New York: Clarion Books, 1988.

Broekel, Ray. *Jet Planes.* Chicago: Children's Press, 1987.

Child, Lydia Maria. Over the River and Through the Woods. New York: Scholastic, 1979.

Chambers, Catherine E. *Flatboats on the Ohio.* Mahwah, New Jersey: Troll Associates, 1986.

♦ Daly, Niki. *Not So Fast, Songololo.* New York: Puffin Books, 1987.

Davidson, Gladys. *Sinbad's Seven Voyages.* New York: Scholastic, 1974.

♦ Dorros, Arthur. *Abuela.* New York: Dutton, 1991.

♦ Dyment, John. *Meet the Men who Sailed the Seas.* New York: Random House, 1966.

♦ Eiseman, Alberta. *Candido.* New York: Macmillan Publishing Co., 1965.

Gobhai, Mehlli. *Ramu and the Kite.* Englewood Cliffs, New Jersey: Prentice Hall, 1986.

Gorsline, Marie and Douglas. *The Pioneers.* New York: Random House, 1978.

Greene, Carol. *Jacques Cousteau, Man of the Oceans.* Chicago: Children's Press, 1990.

Gunston, Bill. *The How and Why Wonder Book of AIRCRAFT.* Los Angeles: Price, Stern, Sloan, 1987.

♦ Hall, Donald. *Ox-Cart Man.* New York: Scholastic, 1979.(A Caldecott Medal Book)

♦ Halpern, Gina. *Where Is Tibet?* Ithaca, New York: Snow Lion Publications, 1991.

♦ Harvey, Brett. *Cassie's Journey.* New York: Holiday House, 1988.

♦ —————— *My Prairie Year.* New York: Holiday House, 1986.

♦ Heide, Florence Parry and Gilliland, Judith Heide. *The Day of Ahmed's Secret.* New York: Scholastic, 1990.

Holling, Clancy. *Paddle to the Sea.* Boston: Houghton Mifflin, 1969. (A Caldecott Honor Book)

Hurwitz, Jane and Sue. *Sally Ride, Shooting for the Stars.* New York: Fawcett Columbine, 1989.

♦ Jassem, Kate. *Sacajawea, Wilderness Guide.* Mahwah, New Jersey: Troll Associates, 1979.

♦ Krensky, Stephen. *Christopher Columbus.* New York: Random House, 1991.

Lauber, Patricia. *Lost Star, The Story of Amelia Earhart.* New York: Scholastic, 1988.

♦ Levine, Ellen. *If You Traveled West in a Covered Wagon.* New York: Scholastic, 1986.

Lewis, Thomas P. *The Dragon Kite.* New York: Holt, Rinehart and Winston, 1974.

♦ Maestro, Betsy. *Snow Day.* New York: Scholastic, 1989.

♦ McGovern, Ann. *If You Lived in Colonial Times.* New York: Scholastic, 1992.

Milsome, John. *Machines in the Air.* Bridgeport, Connecticut: Burke Publishing Co., 1976.

Naden, Corinne J. and Blue, Rose. *Christa McAuliffe, Teacher in Space.* Brookfield, Connecticut: The Millbrook Press, 1991.

Norman, C.J. *Aircraft Carriers*. New York: Franklin Watts, 1986.

◆ Piper, Watty, *The Little Engine that Could*. New York: Monk and Platt, 1961.

Potter, Tony. *Planes*. New York: Macmillan Publishing Co., 1989. (Also available in the same series: *Trucks, Cars,* and *Earth Movers*)

Provensen, Alice and Martin. *The Glorious Flight*. New York: Viking Press, 1983. (A Caldecott Medal Book)

◆ Reynolds, Jan. *Himalaya*. San Diego: Harcourt Brace Javanovich, 1991.

◆ ———— *Sahara*. San Diego: Harcourt Brace Javanovich, 1991.

◆ Robbins, Ken. *Boats*. New York: Scholastic, 1989.

Sabin, Francene. *Amelia Earhart: Adventure in the Sky*. Mahwah, New Jersey: Troll Associates, 1983.

Sabin, Louis. *Wilbur and Orville Wright*. Mahwah, New Jersey: Troll Associates, 1983.

Seuss, Dr. *Oh, the Places You'll Go!* New York: Random House, 1990.

Shannon, Terry. *A Dog Team for Ongluk*. Chicago: Melmont Publishers, 1962.

Siberell, Anne. *a journey to paradise*. New York: Henry Holt & Company, 1990.

Stacy, Tom. *Wings, Wheels, and Sails*. New York: Random House, 1991.

◆ Standiford, Natalie. *The Bravest Dog Ever*. New York: Random House, 1989.

Starr, Susan Breyer. *I Was Good to the Earth Today*. Rohnert Park, California: Staarhouse Publishing with Earth Options Institute, 1992.

Verne, Jules. *Around the World in Eighty Days* (A Longman Structural Reader). New York: Longman, 1976.

◆ Waters, John F., *Camels, Ships of the Desert*. New York: Thomas Y. Crowell, 1974.

◆ Wells, Rosemary. *Abdul*. New York: Dial Books for Young Readers, 1986.

Yep, Laurence. *Dragonwings.* New York: Scholastic, 1990. (A Newbery Honor Book)

Yolen, Jane. *The Emperor and the Kite.* New York: Putnam & Grosset Group (Philomel Books), 1967.

ADDITIONAL RESOURCES

Smallwood, Betty Ansin. *The Literature Connection: A Read-Aloud Guide for Multicultural Classrooms.* Reading, MA: Addison-Wesley, 1991. (This annotated guide to multicultural literature lists additional titles in its section on Community: Transportation/Safety, pages 135–136.)

SPANISH EXPLORERS
VOCABULARY QUIZ

Name_____ Date _____

Fill in the blank with one of the words from the bottom of the page.

1. When we work in teams, consideration and _____ are important.

2. The library is a good place to find _____ on Spanish explorers.

3. Their _____ of the sun at noon helped early explorers follow their route across the ocean.

4. Sailors use a compass for _____.

5. Queen Isabella paid for Columbus's _____ to the New World.

6. Do you remember the _____ of the *La Pinta* on October 12, 1492?

7. In what _____ did Columbus sail?

8. Smallpox caused the death of more than half of the _____ of the Western Hemisphere.

9. What means of _____ did Cortés use in Mexico and Peru?

10. Would you like to be an explorer and lead the _____ of a new country?

cooperation
direction
expedition
exploration
information

location
navigation
observation
population
transportation

RESEARCH QUESTIONS

Name_____ Date _____

1. What was the person's name?

_____

2. Where and when was the person born?

_____

3. In what place or places did the person live?

_____

_____

4. Describe the person's childhood.

_____

_____

_____

5. What education did he or she have?

_____

_____

_____

6. What occupation(s) did the person choose?

_____

_____

_____

RESEARCH QUESTIONS

7. Why did the person become famous?

_____

_____

8. Who was the major influence on the person's life?

_____

_____

9. What were the person's most important accomplishments?

_____

_____

_____

10. Other interesting information:

_____

_____

_____

_____

_____

_____

_____

_____

_____

_____

MULTICULTURAL CELEBRATIONS

Chapter

4

FIESTA, BOUN, AND MELA

CONTENT AREA LEARNING WEB

MULTICULTURAL CELEBRATIONS

SCIENCE

Displaying animal habitats, 104

Creating zoological lotto, 109

MATH

Experimenting with tangrams, 107

LANGUAGE ARTS

Writing announcements, 101

Sampling another foreign language, 103, 104

Writing a script, 103, 108

Conducting interviews, 104

Writing invitations, 104

Writing haiku poetry, 104

Learning origami, 106

Filling out a passport form, 106

Writing a play, 107

FAMILY INVOLVEMENT

Helping with a Multicultural Fair, 100

Teaching calligraphy, 101

Teaching a craft, 101

Lending objects for classroom display, 102

Sharing food with students, 103

Planning a potluck supper, 107

SOCIAL STUDIES

Learning games of other cultures, 101, 103

Learning dances of other cultures, 102, 103

Examining dolls from other countries, 102

Celebrating the Lunar New Year, 103

Making maps, 105

Names from many countries, 105

Discussing occupations, 106

ART AND MUSIC

Making posters, 101, 104

Presenting songs and dances, 101

Making bookmarks and headbands, 101

Designing new currency, 102

Making kites, 104

Making masks, 105

Making a mola, 105

Painting a mural, 105

Listening to international music, 105

Making tissue paper flowers, 108

READING COMPREHENSION

Playing cultural pursuit, 101

Listening to folktales, 103

Researching flags of several countries, 103

Researching totem poles, 108

CHAPTER 4. MULTICULTURAL CELEBRATIONS

Fiesta, Boun, and Mela—no matter where people live or what language they speak, they continue to honor traditions that call for noisy celebrations or quiet, introspective observations. The Spanish word *fiesta* conjures up a colorful festival enlivened by songs, dances, and spicy food. A *boun* is a Laotian festival that has both religious and secular connotations. Bouns are scheduled according to the lunar calendar and are times for reflecting, relaxing, or just plain having fun. In India, a *mela* is a fair that provides an occasion for trade, commerce, entertainment, and relaxation. (One of the best-known melas is the Pushkar Fair, where people come from all over Rajasthan to swim in the sacred lake and to trade camels, sheep, and goats.)

La speranza
E come
La primavera;
Fiorisce
Sempre

Hope is like spring,
it is eternal.

—ITALIAN PROVERB

This chapter outlines ways that you can incorporate these celebrations into your classroom, setting a stage that celebrates diversity all year 'round.

USING A GLOBAL CALENDAR

Presenting a list of celebrations from around the world sets the stage for a discussion of the festivals and religious observations that are important to the students in your class. You'll also find out which of your students may sometimes fast (for example, for Ramadan), and which ones may be absent from time to time (for Lunar New Year or a saint's feast day).

M A T E R I A L S

✓ *"A Global Calendar of Celebrations" reproducible master, pages 111–113*

- Make copies of "A Global Calendar of Celebrations" on pages 111–113 and give each student a copy. Use the calendar as a starting point as you discuss celebrations around the world. Be aware that many events take place on dates determined by lunar and other non-western calendars and thus are found on different dates from year to year.

N O T E

"A Global Calendar of Celebrations" lists only some of the many celebrations held world-wide.

- Ask students to suggest dates that are important to them and have the class add them to their calendars. As each new date is added, ask the student to tell a little about the reason for the holiday and explain how it is observed.

CELEBRATING MULTICULTURAL DIVERSITY

Here are some ways in which you and your students can learn even more about one another's cultures.

- Depending upon the distribution of the student population, you may decide to mark the beginning of the Lunar New Year with an hour-long parade through the school, to celebrate Mexican heritage with a week of activities, or to devote a whole month to Native American cultures. Whatever the activity, what is important is a sustained emphasis on the multicultural diversity in your school and the enrichment it provides to all.

- Another exciting option is to plan an International Week during which your ESL students present a variety of activities for the rest of the school to participate in. If you have the time and energy, you might decide to cap off the year with a large Multicultural Fair which would include songs, dances, food, games, and costumes representing the cultures of all the students in your school. This kind of program requires careful planning and firm commitments from family members. After reading through the listing of possible activities below, you can talk with students about what kind of program they would like to present, and how they might go about preparing for it.

AN ALPHABET OF MULTICULTURAL ACTIVITIES

Here are some multicultural activities, all of which will be of interest to the students, and any of which could be carried out in connection with an International Week or a Multicultural Fair. The list is arranged in alphabetical order. It includes crafts, games, foods, and activities that enable students to share their cultural backgrounds with the class, the school, and the community. It also includes the inevitable logistical and administrative activities, such as the preparation of announcements and invitations.

A

- **Announcements** in various languages can be made by students over the public address system and, in written form, on large, colorful posters made with markers on posterboard or construction paper.

B

- Use a **balloon** theme as the basis of an imaginary flight around the world. Land in the countries your students come from, and have them present typical songs and dances.
- Have students set up an international **bazaar** in which they will sell their (student-made) wares, such as bookmarks, headbands, and hats.
- Ask students to make **bookmarks** using strips of white paper which they decorate with markers. Suggest that students write the words "Read a Book" on them in several languages.

C

MATERIALS

✓ *drawing paper*
✓ *calligraphy pens*

- Invite a family member to come and teach students the art of **calligraphy.**
- Invite family members or volunteers to come and teach a **craft** to students.
- Involve the whole school in a game of **cultural pursuit.** Designate one week during which questions about world geography, history, language, and literature will be answered. Consult with other teachers. Post questions in a central place and provide a shoe box for the answers. Allow for separate sets of questions for Grades 1–2, 3–4, and 5–6. Make sure that students answering questions clearly indicate their names, grades, and, homeroom numbers. Announce winners the next day. Post names of daily winners and overall winners near the school entrance. If possible, give out small prizes or certificates signed by the principal.

READING

✓ Handbook of American Indian Games, *by Allan and Paulette Macfarlan*

- Ask ESL students to teach others to play various string games such as **cat's cradle.** See the *Handbook of American Indian Games,* by Allan and Paulette Macfarlan, for a step-by-step description of this game and other string games.

- Hold a contest aimed at designing a new form of **currency** called the "Unito" for use during the Multicultural Fair. The Unito below was designed by a fifth grade student.

The Unito
Jennifer Arevalo, Age 10

D

- Consult the music and physical education teachers, and enlist their aid in teaching students traditional **dances.** Family members can also be invaluable resources. Popular dances include *El Pajarito,* the Mexican Hat Dance, and the Vietnamese ribbon dance.

- Send home notes inviting family members to lend objects from their countries to be featured in a **display case.** Ask them to be sure to write their names on the objects. Keep an inventory to avoid confusion when you dismantle the display. Dolls, cloth hangings, statuettes, books, and other artifacts make for a colorful multicultural showcase.

✔ Globalchild, *by Maureen Cech*

R E A D I N G

- **Dolls** may be displayed separately if someone is generous enough to lend a personal collection, or if enough people bring dolls from around the world. Cutting out paper dolls is a very popular activity with lower grade students. (*Globalchild,* by Maureen Cech, is a good resource for this activity.)

- Celebrate the Lunar New Year with a **dragon dance, dragon mask,** or **dragon parade** featuring costumes made with the help of students' families.

E

- Schedule an International Week celebration during which students take a compulsory language mini-lesson and two **electives,** choosing from among various international arts, crafts, dances, and games.

F

MATERIALS

✓ costumes from students' native countries
✓ still camera or videotaping equipment

- Organize an international **fashion show.** Let students write their script and appoint a (student) fashion coordinator to supervise the details. Schedule several dress rehearsals. Take pictures or make a video of the show.

- Encourage students to research and recreate **flags** of designated countries. Hang them at the entrance of the school, in the school cafeteria, or in your classroom.

- Set up a Multicultural Reading Corner in your classroom (or in the library, if possible). Ask the librarian to read aloud international **folktales** and/or **fairy tales** during the fair.

- Family members are usually very eager to share native-country **foods** with the rest of the school. However, school policies vary from one school district to another, so it is best to clear such a plan with school administrators beforehand.

- **Fortune cookies** make a great snack for Lunar New Year, if a family will donate them or your school can afford to buy them.

G

- Coordinate with the physical education teacher and ask family members for help in setting up **games** for students to play during the fair. You might feature games such as *Chopsticks and Lemon* from Cambodia, *Yute* from Korea, *O An Quan* from Vietnam, and *Go* from Japan. International Week is a golden opportunity for ESL students to teach some of these games to native English speakers and gain prestige in their eyes.

✓ *long, narrow scraps of white cloth*
✓ *fabric paints or markers*

H

- Transform your classroom into a living museum. See Volume 1, Chapter 3 for ideas on animals and their **habitats** that you might feature.

- Teach students how to make **headbands.** Take an old piece of cloth or sheeting and divide it into long, narrow strips. Invite students to paint and decorate them. They can then be sold or traded at the bazaar.

- Ask students to compare and contrast various versions of **hopscotch.** Encourage them to write the rules, assisted by peers or family members. Special versions of hopscotch may then be taught to native English speakers by their ESL peers.

I

- Ask native speakers to **interview** ESL students about their personal experiences and about their native countries and write up the results for the school paper. Always stress the fact that ESL students constitute a valuable resource for the school and the community.

- Send **invitations** to families, volunteers, and other people in the community to attend the Multicultural Fair.

J

- Invite students to compare and contrast the way in which they use the jump rope. Then have them teach each other new ways to **jump rope.**

K

- Ask students to make **kites.** This activity, and a discussion of Kite Day in Japan, can also lead to the writing of haiku poetry.

L

- Ask ESL students to give **language lessons** to their peers and to teachers. Suggest that they pick out some basic greetings and vocabulary and write the words on a poster along with accompanying pictures, if they wish. Have them teach one small group at a time. Encourage family members to help out, if they are available.

- Make **lanterns** out of paper as part of a crafts session. These can also be made in conjunction with the Lantern Festival listed on the Global Calendar.

M

- Invite students to bring in **maps** of their countries of origin. Post a large map on the wall and show the various countries represented in the classroom or in the school. Use maps to pinpoint the itinerary followed by the imaginary balloon flight suggested in the "B" activities on its trip around the world.

- Invite students to bring **marbles** and compare ways in which they play marbles.

- Students can make **masks** in connection with a variety of activities, from celebrating holidays to imitating animals.

MATERIALS

✓ construction paper
✓ scissors
✓ glue
✓ mola or a picture of a mola

- The Cuna Indians of the San Blaz Islands in Panama are famous for their beautiful *molas,* which consist of appliqué work on the front of blouses. Prepare piles of colored construction paper in vivid hues of red, green, yellow, and black. Cut out construction paper frames, allowing one frame for three pieces of paper. Show students molas or pictures of molas. Invite them to design their own and select the experts who will then become teachers and guide other students as they make their own. (*Globalchild,* by Maureen Cech provides detailed instructions on making molas.)

MATERIALS

✓ butcher paper
✓ paint
✓ paintbrushes

- During International Week, **murals** lend a festive look to the classroom or the school. Children learn much in the process of making them. Agree on a theme, provide butcher paper, paintbrushes, and paints, and let them go to work.

- Use **music** to provide a backdrop of international sound to your students' presentations. Consult with the music teacher, family members, and outsiders for advice and as a source of tapes.

N

- The proper use of **names** can be the object of a mini-lesson. For instance, if you have a number of Lao students in the school, you might have some of the more advanced ones explain the source of many Lao names: flowers (*Chanthava* means *gardenia*), precious metals (*Bak Kham* means *gold*), and bright colors (*Bak Deng* means *red*).

O

M
A
T
E
R
I
A
L
S

✓ colorful yarn
✓ twigs or tongue depressors

- Invite family members to come to class and talk about the **occupations** they had in their countries. Encourage them to teach the class a craft or a skill.

- Have students who know how to make one teach the rest of the class how to make an **Ojo de Dios.** Maureen Cech gives clear, simple instructions for constructing these colorful stick and yarn decorations in *Globalchild.* Hang the completed "Eyes of God" from the ceiling.

- Most Chinese, Korean, and Japanese students know **origami,** the art of paper folding. Origami paper can be found in craft or hobby stores and instructions are usually included in the packet of papers.

P

✓ Ranger Rick *magazine,* January 1990

R
E
A
D
I
N
G

M
A
T
E
R
I
A
L
S

✓ "Passport" reproducible master, page 114

- Make **paper puffer fish.** Use the January 1990 issue of *Ranger Rick* magazine to teach your students how to make these impressive folded-paper fish.

- Have students create **passports,** including a number, pertinent information, and visas for the countries they "visit." As students complete activities during International Week or visit various booths at the Multicultural Fair, ask them to write in the requested information and have their passports stamped by the person in charge. You can use the "Passport" reproducible on page 114 or make up your own format. If you use the reproducible, fold the copy in half once lengthwise and then once the other way to form a four-page passport booklet which students can write in.

- Recycle leftover **photocopy paper** whenever possible to help conserve trees.

- No celebration of Las Posadas is complete without a *piñata.* For instructions, see *Globalchild,* by Maureen Cech.

- Ask students to write and act out **plays** based on some of the folktales you have read to them. They will learn about dialogue, proper use of quotation marks, etc. If lower grade students are involved in these plays, ask some upper grade students to be the narrators. They can also help design the sets, create props, and rehearse for the big moment.

- If you are allowed to bring food into your school, there is no better way to cement friendship and mutual understanding than by sponsoring a **potluck supper.** Invite families to bring favorite dishes from their native countries. Label each dish to show what it contains and where it comes from.

- Let the community hear what is going on in your school by using **press releases.** Locate the contacts at your local newspaper and send out information well in advance telling about activities you wish the community to participate in.

Q

- Be sure to have large **quantities** of game materials, crafts supplies, and food on hand for your celebration.

R

✓ *long pieces of ribbon*
✓ *tall, stable pole*

- Most Vietnamese or Chinese students will know the intricate steps of the **ribbon dance,** which always delights audiences. Record it on videotape if possible.

S

- **Schedule** time for your celebration well in advance. The school calendar is usually very crowded, and it may not be a bad idea to sign up for a spot a year ahead of time.

T

- **Tangrams** were invented thousands of years ago by a Chinese man named Tan. These puzzles consist of seven pieces which fit together to make designs, such as animal shapes. (See Volume 1, Chapter 3.) A tangram table is always a popular activity at a Multicultural Fair.

- **Tissue paper flowers** are easy to make and lend color to any celebration. Girls often like to wear them in their hair, too.

- **Totem poles** are especially appropriate for a celebration of Native American heritage. Encourage students to try building them out of a variety of materials. They can even start with a stack of recycled plastic jugs.

- Suggest that students make a map and prepare a **tour** of their countries which they will later present to groups of students during International Week. Revise the script, have them practice with partners, and provide a pointer which they can use to single out points of interest on a map.

U

- Consider inviting a community member to show pictures and talk to students about the role of the **United Nations** in helping people around the world.

V

MATERIALS

✔ photocopied "visas"
✔ foam trays
✔ carving knives
✔ ink pads
✔ "Passport" reproducible master, page 114

- Create **visas** for students to use as they go from one activity to another during the Multicultural Fair. This will encourage them to experience a variety of different cultures. Create a clear, simple visa format and reproduce copies for all students. If you wish, you can use the visa section on the "Passport" reproducible on page 114. For stamps, you can experiment with seals carved from recycled foam trays and pressed on ink pads. Assign students to various stations to check passports, fill in visa information, and stamp the visas. This way, you are creating jobs and keeping everybody happy and occupied.

W

- **Wildflowers** make pretty decorations and sales items for the Multicultural Fair.

X

- Counteract **xenophobia** by helping students, family members, and other teachers understand the important contributions made by all foreign cultures to life in the United States.

Y

- Invite students to join you for a few quiet moments of **yoga** relaxation between the bustle of various activities. Ask students to lie on the floor, bring their knees to their chests, and rest their tired backs in *Tadasana,* the mountain pose.

Z

- Play **zoological lotto.** Help students make up a lotto game using the names of various zoo animals. This board game can give students a chance to sit down and focus on a quiet activity after taking part in more active projects.

CONCLUSION

The Multicultural Fair promotes socialization among ESL students, increases their self-confidence, reinforces multicultural awareness in the school and the community, and expands the horizons of all who participate in it. All the activities presented in this chapter and throughout the two volumes of *The Global Classroom* are meant to encourage you to design your own curriculum units. All suggestions are based on the premise that cultural diversity offers opportunities for enrichment, that each student's experience is authentic and valid, and that we all are links in an immense circle of interconnectedness.

SUGGESTED READINGS

(Titles mentioned in this chapter are marked with a ♦.)

Allen, Judy, McNeill, Earldene, and Schmidt, Velma. *Cultural Awareness for Children.* Menlo Park, California: Addison-Wesley, 1992.

Carlson, Laurie. *Ecoart.* Charlotte, Vermont: Williamson Publishing, 1993.

♦ Cech, Maureen. *Globalchild.* Reading, Massachusetts: Addison-Wesley, 1991.

Chan, Barbara J. *KidPix™ Around the World: A Multicultural Computer Activity Book.* Reading, Massachusetts: Addison-Wesley, 1993.

Goldstein, Peggy. *Long is a Dragon: Chinese Writing for Children.* New York: Scholastic, 1991.

Lee, Kay and Marsall, eds. *The Illuminated Book of Days.* New York: G.P. Putnam's Sons, 1979.

MacDonald, Margaret Read. *Peace Tales.* Hamden, Connecticut: Linnet Books, 1992.

♦ Macfarlan, Allan and Paulette. *Handbook of American Indian Games.* New York: Dover Publications, 1958.

Milford, Susan. *Hands Around the World: 365 Ways to Build Cultural Awareness and Global Respect.* Charlotte, Vermont: Williamson Publishing, 1992.

Mundahl, John. *Tales of Courage, Tales of Dreams.* Reading, Massachusetts: Addison-Wesley, 1993.

OTHER RESOURCES

♦ *Ranger Rick,* January 1990. (Directions for making paper puffer fish)

A GLOBAL CALENDAR OF CELEBRATIONS

(If no date is given, the exact day—and sometimes month—varies from year to year.)

Month	Date	Celebration	Celebrated by
January	1	New Year	Countries world-wide
	6	Epiphany (Three Kings' Day)	Christian people
	14	Beginning of kite season	India
	15	Martin Luther King, Jr.'s birthday	U.S.A.
	20	Babin Den (Grandmother's Day)	Bulgaria
		Lunar New Year	Asian people
		Alacitas (Festival for the Aymara god of prosperity)	Bolivia
February	14	Valentine's Day	U.S.A.
		Losar (Lunar New Year)	Tibet
		Black History Month	U.S.A.
		Carnival/Mardi Gras (Beginning of Lent)	Latin countries: France, Italy, Portugal, Spain, Latin America, the Caribbean, Goa
		Fasching (Shrove Tuesday)	Bavaria (in Germany), Austria
March	21	Nouruz (New Year)	Iran
	25	Independence Day	Greece
		Hina Matsuri (Doll festival)	Japan
		Ramadan (Beginning of fast)	Islamic people
		Holi (Spring festival of colors)	Hindu people
April	12–15	Pi Mai (Lao New Year)	Laos, Cambodia
	13–15	Buddhist New Year	Buddhist people in Southeast Asia
	22	Earth Day	Countries world-wide
		Id al-Fitr (End of fast)	Islamic people
		Passover	Jewish people
		Easter	Christian people

A GLOBAL CALENDAR
OF CELEBRATIONS

(If no date is given, the exact day—and sometimes month—varies from year to year.)

Month	Date	Celebration	Celebrated by
May	1	May Day, Labor Day	European countries
	5	Cinco de Mayo (Defeat of Napolean II and the French)	Mexico
	5	Tango no sekku (Boys' festival)	Japan
	17	Nasjonaldagen (Constitution Day)	Norway
	25	African Freedom Day	African countries
		Asian-Pacific Heritage Week	U.S.A.
June	12	Independence Day	Philippines
	24	Midsummer's Eve	Sweden, Norway, Spain, Paraguay
		Native American "powwows" (through September)	Canada, U.S.A.
July	1	Dominion Day	Canada
	4	Independence Day	U.S.A.
	7	Tanabata (Star festival)	Japan
	14	Bastille Day	France
	24	Simón Bolívar's birthday	Latin America
	25	Santiago Apostol (St. James's Day)	Spain
		Beginning of Lent	Buddhist people
August	15	Assumption Day	Catholic people
		August Moon	China
		Feast of St. Anthony	Italy
		Independence Day	India

A GLOBAL CALENDAR OF CELEBRATIONS

(If no date is given, the exact day—and sometimes month—varies from year to year.)

Month	Date	Celebration	Celebrated by
September	16	Independence Day	Mexico
		Water Festival (End of rainy season)	Laos
		Lantern Festival	Vietnam
		Id al Mawlid (Mohammed's birthday)	Islamic countries
		Rosh Hashanah (Jewish New Year)	Jewish people
		Hispanic Heritage Month (starts 9/15)	U.S.A.
		New Year's Day	Ethiopia
October	2	Mahatma Ghandi's birthday	India
	24	United Nations Day	Countries world-wide
	31	Halloween	U.S.A.
		Alphabet Day	Korea
		Dussehra, Dassain (10-day festivals of Durga Puja)	Hindu people of India, Nepal
November	1–2	All Saints' Day, All Souls' Day	Catholic people
		Diwali (Festival of lights)	Hindu people
		Thanksgiving	U.S.A.
		Nanak Devji's birthday	Sikh people
		Kiougou (Harvest celebration)	Burkina Faso (formerly Upper Volta)
December	1	St. Nicholas Day	Europe
	13	St. Lucia's Day	Sweden
	16–25	La Posadas (Nine nights of Christmas)	Mexico
	25	Christmas	Catholic people
		Kwanzaa	African Americans
		Hanukkah (Festival of lights)	Jewish people
		Harvest Celebration	Laos

UNITED NATIONS PASSPORT

Number _____

NAME _____ (first) _____ (last)

BIRTH DATE _____ (month/day/year)

☐ MALE ☐ FEMALE

HEIGHT ____ feet ____ inches

BIRTHPLACE

HAIR COLOR

EYE COLOR

STREET ADDRESS

APT. NO.

CITY

STATE

ZIP

NATIONALITY

DATE OF ISSUE _____ (month/day/year)

SIGNATURE OF BEARER

VISA

Country: _____

Date of entry: _____

ACTIVITY

_____
_____
_____

VISA

Country: _____

Date of entry: _____

ACTIVITY

_____
_____
_____

VISA

Country: _____

Date of entry: _____

ACTIVITY

_____
_____
_____

VISA

Country: _____

Date of entry: _____

ACTIVITY

_____
_____
_____

114

Peace

Peace is our friend.
It is what we all want to have.
Peace is our future.
It's our life.
Without peace,
We won't be alive.

Many kids do not know
What the word "peace" means.
And there is no one to tell them,
Because none of these people know what it is.

They only know what war is.
The dark, killing enemy that no one can stop.

And who made war?
You people!
It's you, that darkness.
You're the war.
You kill poor people without homes.
But why? Don't you have other things to do?
Why kill? War isn't what we need.
Don't you see?
We need peace! That's what we need.
To keep the peace, our friend.
Peace is what we all need to have.

Stanislava Uhrik, Age 11